FIRE IN THE EYES OF YOUTH:

The Humanities in American Education

FIRE IN THE EYES OF YOUTH:

The Humanities in American Education

Edited by Randolph Jennings
Introduction by Judith Rényi

Occasional Press
St. Paul

The programs of CHART, and the publication of this book, have been supported through grants from the Rockefeller Foundation. The opinions expressed are those of the individual authors, and do not neccesarily reflect the views of the Rockefeller Foundation, CHART, or the Occasional Press.

Editorial assistance from Patricia Weaver Francisco and Deborah Johnson.

Designed by Barbara Redmond Design, Inc.

Additional design and production services by Stanton Publication Services, Inc.

Interior illustrations by Jeremy Schnorr and Keith Schmiedlin. These drawings were created in 1988–89, when both were eighth-grade students.

ISBN: 0–939962-10–1

To order additional copies, send $10 plus $3.00 postage & handling to:

    Occasional Press

    558 Lincoln Avenue

    St. Paul, MN 55102–2815

Please note: All orders must be prepaid by check or money order. Minnesota residents please add $.65 sales tax. To order multiple copies, please write for discount information.

Acknowledgements and Dedication

We are grateful to the school superintendents and principals who have supported these experiments in teaching and learning, and to the many partners from businesses and foundations throughout the country who have made this work possible.

A very special thanks is due to Alberta B. Arthurs and Steven Lavine, discoverers of great teachers and teaching in many of these sites, and to Hugh B. Price for carrying on the good work.

Fire in the Eyes of Youth was generously supported by a grant from The Rockefeller Foundation, which initiated CHART and has provided vital support to the projects since 1983. To the directors and staffs of these projects we express our appreciation for their hard work, their dedication, and their abiding faith in the minds of children. We are also very grateful for the tireless work of the countless artists, writers, museum curators, scholars, poets, and storytellers who have contributed to student learning in these projects. To all those who have labored, we offer our heartfelt thanks.

Above all, we wish to thank the thousands of students and hundreds of teachers who have cheerfully gone to work to read and write and explore cultures old and new, and have thereby created vibrant, important classrooms. To these students, their parents, and their communities we dedicate this book in our continuing quest to help them make connections and discoveries about themselves and all of us.

Contents

Descriptions of CHART Projects   123

The Arts and Humanities in American Education
Judith Rényi

In the early 1980s a host of government and private studies of American education began to appear painting a devastating portrait of our nation's public schools. The Department of Education charged that we lived in a "nation at risk" because of our schools' inability to prepare our young people for the complex lives they would face as adults in the new millennium. Others described systems of teacher preparation and school organization that were inadequate to the task of enabling education professionals to improve the schools.

Among the reports of 1980 was a study commissioned by the Rockefeller Foundation, *The Humanities in American Life*, that set out not to examine education, but to portray instead a picture of the fortunes of history and literature, philosophy, and art and music as they were understood and enjoyed by the American public at large. The commission concluded that these areas of our culture were strongly alive and well only in isolated institutions, such as museums and universities, but that their future was at risk because average American school children received little exposure to them in their schooling.

While it is exceedingly difficult to succinctly define "the humanities" and their importance to America, let us turn to the definition used in the 1980 Rockefeller Foundation report:

> Through the humanities we reflect on the fundamental question: what does it mean to be human? The humanities offer clues but never a complete answer. They reveal how people have tried to make moral, spiritual, and intellectual sense of a world in which irrationality, despair, loneliness, and death are as conspicuous as birth, friendship, hope, and reason. We learn how individuals or societies define the moral life and try to attain it, attempt to reconcile freedom and the responsibilities of citizenship, and express themselves artistically. The humanities do not necessarily mean humaneness, nor do they always inspire the individual with what Cicero called "incentives to noble action." But by awakening a sense of what it might be like to be someone else or to live in another time or culture, they tell us about ourselves, stretch our imagination, and enrich our experience. They increase our distinctively human potential.
>
> The humanities presume particular methods of expression and inquiry—language, dialogue, reflection, imagination, and metaphor. In the humanities the aims of these

Judith Rényi is director of Collaboratives for Humanities and Arts Teaching (CHART). Established by the Rockefeller Foundation, CHART helps teachers strengthen multicultural and international education in public schools. Locally created and implemented programs are currently in operation across the nation, in eleven urban and three statewide rural locations.

Illustration by Keith Schmiedlin.

activities of mind are not geometric proof and quantitative measure, but rather insight, perspective, critical understanding, discrimination, and creativity. These aims are not unique to the humanities, but are found in other fields, in images from the arts, and in new forms of expression created by film, television and computers. No matter how large their circle, however, the humanities remain dedicated to the disciplined development of verbal, perceptual, and imaginative skills needed to understand experience.

The Humanities in American Life (Berkeley: University of California Press, 1980), pp. 1–2.

What becomes clear from such language is that the study of "the humanities" fosters a dialogue among students and the voices of writers and vision of artists and thoughts of historians, philosophers, and other interpreters, that should begin in school and continue all one's life as one struggles endlessly to come to terms—always provisional—with the human condition. Such dialogue is essential both to individual identity and autonomy and to one's capacity to negotiate the personal, social, moral, civic, and working world. The humanities in such a definition are neither "soft," nor "impractical," nor "enrichment." They are the bedrock of an education in a civil society. Embedded in this definition is the notion that the humanities always put us in touch with other voices from our own or other cultures. In this sense, the humanities are by their very nature multicultural.

The Rockefeller Foundation concluded on the basis of this study that support for a lively life in the humanities for all Americans depended on a vigorous engagement with reading and writing and cultures in all of our schools. Collaboratives for Humanities and Arts Teaching (CHART) was created and funded by the Rockefeller Foundation as an effort to develop classrooms where such an education could take place. Classrooms of average students from impoverished urban and rural districts were chosen as the target sites for this work because the commissioned study expressed particular concern that the young adults emerging from these schools had had little previous contact with powerful uses of language, historical understanding, or the joy of struggling with complex ideas and arguments.

The picture of the average classroom in large, urban schools as well as in smaller, rural ones consists far too often of what Martin Haberman calls the "pedagogy of poverty."[1] For many years educators believed that there were "basics" in learning—the mechanics of reading and writing, vocabulary, grammar, and calculation—that needed to be mastered first, thereby providing the student with isolated skills that could then be used to build toward more complex thinking and learning. Therefore, schools spent considerable time and effort, especially in the first through eighth grades, drilling skills. Students received work sheets and filled them out, day in and day out. Teachers asked questions only in order to hear answers preordained by the teachers' manual. There were only right or wrong answers, and the business of children was to learn to repeat the right ones.

This pedagogy prevails most often in schools where children are poor and least often in schools for those of the greatest privilege. In urban and rural settings children encounter educators who lament students' impoverished vocabularies, their lack of "reading readiness," their "culture of poverty" or of "otherness."

A basic "drill-for-skill" education is, unfortunately, rather boring. In such classrooms one reads a story only in order to answer the teacher's questions, the story in question chooses vocabulary primarily for didactic purposes rather than aesthetic ones, and the story line depends for its events more on grammar than on plot. In such classrooms history is a set of right answers and formulaic understandings (such as the three—and only three—causes of the Civil War, all of which are known and easily defined). Such classrooms are intellectually stifling for everyone, but distinctly dangerous for students who may not encounter alternative modes of thought outside of the classroom. In addition, in such classes children whose cultural backgrounds differ significantly from that of the school culture are told they have *no* language, or are culturally deficient, with virtually every word the child tries to express.

Although the basic skills approach is both boring and punitive for children, most still learn to play the school game well enough to graduate, but many students are unwilling to play a game they see as merely tedious, irrelevant, and denigrating. For these students, mental dropping out begins as early as the third grade, when it begins to become clear that nothing new or exciting is going to vary the routine of drill.

The humanities in all their power and richness of spirit are not present in a basic skills education. Children alienated by six or eight years of basics often don't bother learning to read at all. If reading is only ever presented as something trivial or dull, there is no incentive to become a good reader. If everyone already knows all the right answers about history, and if that history lesson never honors the child's own questions or hypotheses, there is no incentive to become just one more parrot in the chorus. Children so turned away from using their innately inquiring minds after years of mindless schooling will arrive in high school unprepared to take on the humanities on offer there. A child who cannot read well by ninth grade and who has had little or no previous experience of literature written for aesthetic rather than grammatical purposes will only be puzzled by the usually obligatory *Julius Caesar*. Ninth grade usually also offers a one-year, rather breathless romp through world history from the Ice Ages to World War I, with few stops by the wayside to acknowledge the existence of Africa or Asia or Latin America—the homelands of many of the children in present-day urban classrooms.

A self-fulfilling prophecy takes hold in the pedagogy of poverty. Basic skills are offered; students find them tedious and fail to learn them; basic skills are offered again and again relentlessly in repeated efforts to *force* children to learn them; the humanities (the higher order, complex learning) get put off indefinitely; and the students never get a chance to read real books, understand real history, or grapple with the questions and problems that have intrigued and beguiled humanity for thousands of years or with the imaginative and thoughtful and tough responses humanity has wrought over the ages and in different places in order to think about these questions and problems.

That is the picture CHART set out to alter in the early 1980s. The Rockefeller Foundation had substantial experience in supporting the arts and humanities in museums and universities and through fellowships to artists and researchers, but none in the area of changing the way large public school systems operate. The Foundation sought ways of supporting teachers as agents of change, since this approach most closely resembled their experience in supporting individual academics and artists in the past. But teachers were far less autonomous than academics or artists. They were deeply embedded in complex systems. To say that you want to see average children in urban schools learning a rich, demanding new curriculum and that you will accomplish this change by investing in teachers' professional growth is to ignore the contextual system and what amounts to a need for social engineering on an immense scale.

The model for change we began with went something like this: Teachers themselves can change what happens in their classrooms if given enough knowledge, opportunity, and resources. Therefore, we must provide extensive learning experiences for teachers, introduce them to new humanities knowledge and expertise, and then provide them the permission and opportunity to use their new knowledge in the schoolroom. The result will be students who learn the humanities—who will read more and write more and know more about diverse cultures.

We were profoundly naive when we imagined this model. There were so many realities of schooling we did not take into consideration that we have only now, after nearly a decade of work, begun to realize how much we didn't know and how much yet remains to be done to substitute real humanities for basic skills in the schools.

In the typical CHART project, a superintendent working with the leadership of a local education fund representing the business and cultural interests of the city, decides that the curriculum of the schools needs more student writing or more non-Western history or more diverse arts programming. The local education fund raises grant support from local corporations and foundations and perhaps the National Endowment for the Humanities as well as the Rockefeller Foundation. With amounts from $250,000 to $1 million in such support committed per year for three years, depending on the size of the district being served, the local education fund calls on local artists or historians, museum curators or storytellers to put together an intensive summer institute, where a few teachers from each of a dozen schools will study history or literature or multicultural arts.

Armed with this new knowledge, the cadre of teachers from each school plans a new curriculum, which often turns out to be interdisciplinary. Interdisciplinary ideas might include such things as subject matter in the English, social studies, and art classes, for instance, carefully coordinated around a shared theme or central idea of study, such as "human migration" or "coming-of-age stories and practices" or "urbanization" or "the development of metalworking in different cultures." And then, having developed this new idea, all the teachers have to do is teach it and all will be well.

From the start, CHART teachers themselves immediately began to teach *us* what really needed to happen to transform the pedagogy of poverty into a classroom of intellectual riches. They reminded us that we had considered only two pieces of the classroom puzzle: subject matter and teachers' knowledge of it. They told us that pedagogy itself, the method of teaching, was the third indispensable piece necessary to form a new picture. It was perfectly possible to give teachers exciting new knowledge about African bronze sculpture or Puerto Rican poetry or documents on migration written by native Americans, and still have the teachers turn all of that into drill-for-skill work sheets. Without a transformation of teaching methods, all the wonderful knowledge itself would remain no different from that of the old curriculum: trivial, dull, and inert.

Teachers also taught us that public school systems and the state bureaucracies and legislation that sanction their existence place high value on the results of tests that ensure right answers rather than good arguments, final answers rather than tentative questions, and short answers rather than extended argument or fine discriminations. Teachers dutiful to such demands would drop the experimental project for two weeks so as to drill their students in the material coming up on the state test.

Teachers told us they didn't have enough time. Not enough time in a forty-two minute period to dig into a subject; not enough time to take a class to a museum; not enough time to talk to their colleagues to plan a coordinated curriculum; not enough time to read 150 essays a week the students ought to be writing; not enough time to absorb their own new learning, develop a curriculum (which they'd never before been asked to do), and get it to fit into a school year that was already overstuffed with a breathless required romp through the history of the world.

The artists and academics who worked with the teachers knew their subjects well but didn't know how to imagine pedagogies appropriate to developing inquiring minds. They often treated teachers the way teachers treated kids: they just lectured, telling teachers the truth as they saw it, asking inauthentic questions to which they already knew the answers, answering teachers' questions authoritatively so as to establish that their own expertise was superior to that of the teachers.

Struggling through all of these problems, we learned from teachers that we had grabbed hold of a very small toe of a very large fire-breathing dragon. The schools could not be changed this way. The humanities could not fight their way into a real place in the curriculum without massive changes in the ways the schools operated.

What did work, in introducing a profoundly new and important way of teaching the arts in Pittsburgh, or creating teams of teachers to sustain learning across subject areas in Los Angeles, or developing an entirely new, genuinely international, world history curriculum in Philadelphia, were some key understandings and agreements among the powers in each of those places. Superintendents had to help create "safe havens" for experimentation to occur; principals had to pave the way for 150 high school students to be "block" scheduled to a single group of four teachers at a particular class time, instead of being scattered willy-nilly among the dozens of other teachers in the school. Standardized tests, where inappropriate to the new learning, had to be suspended; teachers were invited to imagine more appropriate assessments. Above all else, these projects had the sustained help of agencies outside the schools. These agencies had been invited by the school superintendents to work in close partnership with them to reform the curriculum. The depth and seriousness of such sustained partnerships are critical to new ideas entering into the schools. Business leaders, university presidents, researchers, local foundations, cultural and civic agencies all joined hands with superintendents to fund, support, evaluate, and oversee implementation of the successful programs.

Teachers are intrepid creatures who managed to make extraordinary things happen in their classrooms despite the opposition of the inert mass of the system. A group of teacher in rural South Carolina got their students to write about the crafts practiced in their region from time immemorial. One sixteen-year-old, whose test scores repeatedly labeled him as near-illiterate, produced a well-written thirty-page essay on sweet grass basket weaving that linked his mother's and grandmother's and great-grandmother's basket patterns to similar pieces to be found in a museum exhibition from Ghana. This student demonstrated a deep understanding of art history, and through that art history learned of his own family's probable homeland in Africa. Such work is genuinely a contribution to the humanities. The student so empowered to question, research, and argue a case about the arts of his own family and community provides for us all a new example of a link across time.

In a Philadelphia inner-city classroom where some tenth-graders can't read, the new world history curriculum starts in the deep prehistoric past with a series of cutout cardboard models of skulls. The students are asked to group themselves in fours and fives to examine the model skulls and decide on the basis of evidence and hypothesis which belonged to prehominids, and which to *Homo sapiens*. Each group presents its agreed-on argument to the whole class, and after extended debate the class comes to consensus. They then invariably demand to know from the teacher, "What's the *real* answer?" She tells them: the same arguments they've just used are being made in the pages of learned archaeological journals, and no consensus exists. The students have enacted a highly sophisticated, current, and hotly debated controversy about the prehistorical development of our species.

In a classroom in San Francisco twenty immigrant students from as many countries group in twos to interview each other about their life histories. Each writes a biography of her partner; the partner reads and edits, and the pair discusses needed changes. Each student depends on understanding the other as he tells the life story. Each must clarify her English usage so as to be understood. The biographies are a poignant testament to the individual's need to express and to be understood.

And in St. Paul a poet sits among kindergartners and asks them for language with which to write a poem. The children choose a theme together and compose a long, long poem about a long, long snake. The poet writes down all the children's words, and then they all troop to the computer lab to print it up and revise it together. These five-year-olds have no problem with writing or reading or "difficult" words. In fact, the longer the word, the better, for this long, long snake.

Above all, a student in Miami writes a poem about the American flag demonstrating the power of old symbols made new through his special insights into language. Kenric Leach's "Red, White and Blue" gave us the title of this book, and uses disturbing and powerful language for understanding American diversity. When students write their own way into the curriculum like this, we know we have succeeded.

Such scenes as these have happened in hundreds of classrooms around the nation for thousands of children in the ten years of CHART's efforts to introduce humanities to the public schools. We have confirmed our own beliefs in the children in every case. In the Los Angeles HUMANITAS project, for instance, inner-city children randomly selected for the program emerged after a year or two ready for advanced placement, college-level work. Students who had never written well or extensively before rose to the occasion to write extended arguments and good poetry. Students who never saw much of worth in school now think of themselves as researchers and plan on going to college. Students' attendance went up, and yes, even those dreaded test scores went up.

These kinds of results have been seen among all kinds of students from all kinds of backgrounds. Poverty of pocket does not mean poverty of mind or will. Students whose own cultures have never before been honored by school, have found their own voice by reading the works of great writers such as Toni Morrison or Etheridge Knight. Students who silently drifted through years of a schooling of passivity took an active part in constructing their own knowledge.

But in our efforts to transform curricula in public schools we found the humanities subjects themselves were not enough, nor were the newly enfranchised teachers enough. We also needed powerful pedagogies, safe havens from punitive tests, and time to prove that average urban and rural students could indeed produce work that not only they but the society at large could value.

The Role of Schooling in American Life

The single largest barrier to getting the humanities to flourish in public schools may come eventually from the very definition of those schools as institutions designed to effect social rather than intellectual development. Such institutions depend on social science rather than humanistic ideas and methods. America looks to its public schools as the central agency for social transformation. The public schools are where new immigrants shed their old ways to become Americans—their old language, habits, and beliefs are to be discarded and the use of English, middle-class manners and the democratic way of life are to be taken on, primarily in school. School is also believed to be the primary agency for democratic equity. It is in school that rich and poor, black and white learn to believe in America and American economic and political ideas.

The place of the public school as the single most important social agency in America becomes apparent when we think how easily and strongly public opinion is roused whenever any proposed changes to this near-sacred institution are proposed. Moreover, when social ills plague us, we turn to the schools more often than to any other institution to correct them. If drugs or crime or disease stalk our land, we are quick to identify a need for better or new or more education. Social legislation more often results in public school mandates than in any other form of social transformation.

Public schools are therefore the solution of first resort for social change, and America thinks of its public schools as social agencies. The social sciences have therefore naturally dominated school practices for many years. Children's developmental psychology and the cognitive sciences that seek to understand how people learn are foremost among the subjects taught and researched in teacher-preparation programs. Social sciences inform and define the interactions between teachers and students—the instructional methods teachers study in college; and social science prevails in describing how schools should be organized and function as well as evaluating how well students, teachers, and schools perform.

Since public schools are indeed social institutions, and perhaps the only such institutions in America controlled by government, they express our best hopes for and largest investment in a democratic America. But the social science dominance of teacher preparation, schooling, and testing may also have another effect, which is to misunderstand or even neglect the intellectual development of children.

Pragmatic America prefers that children learn to read well enough to read the newspaper and calculate well enough to balance a checkbook. But to aim for such goals is to aim very low, and to aim low is to value a child's mind inadequately. A child's aspirations are limitless. Reading could answer these aspirations by opening up limitless possibilities. And so it is with each of the subjects of the liberal arts—with History and Science and Mathematics as well as Literature. There is, therefore, a structural conflict in American schooling, between the social science dominance of teacher preparation, instructional methods, and testing and the intellectual development through the liberal arts that ostensibly take up much of the instructional time in school.

The Value of the Humanities

Ultimately what happens is that literature is taught not for the sake of either enjoyment or exploration of ideas or for developing students' engagement with well-wrought language, but to improve students' social needs, such as behavior, manners (including and primarily good grammar), and beliefs (particularly political and patriotic). History is taught not to develop students' analytical skills or even knowledge of the past so much as to provide a minimal belief system in American ideologies. Such purposes are more often evident in schools where little intellectual capacity among students is expected. In these classrooms so little intellectual development is taught that these low expectations are in fact fulfilled.

Enabling the humanities to gain a toehold in such a hostile environment is the goal we set ourselves when we announced our intention of strengthening humanities education in public schools where large numbers of poor and minority students predominate. The essays that follow show a number of teachers struggling with these issues. The school environments, state regulations, and teachers' own backgrounds tend very strongly to *use* the humanities in the service of social rather than intellectual ends.

It is often very difficult even to introduce humanities-centered classrooms at all. Such classrooms would have as their hallmark the study of "texts"—and a text is not a text*book*. A text could be a poem or novel, it could be an historical document such as a Native American diary recording a personal view of the onslaught of European settlers, or it could be the Declaration of Independence. A text might be a work of art, a passage from the Bible or the Koran or Confucian proverbs, or a ceremonial dance or a procession. All of these and an infinite number of other materials produced by human beings in this or any culture at any time could be the central text.

A text alone, however, does not ensure a "humanities" course of study, unless that text is then analyzed and understood using the methods of the major humanities disciplines. Historians "read" texts differently from scientists, although both have much in common. Both have a concern for the evidence and the context in which the evidence appears; both construct logical arguments based on evidence; both must write or describe verbally their arguments to persuade others of the value of their interpretations. But historians characteristically study human action over time and seek to understand human interactions and motivations, while scientists characteristically study the physical actions and behaviors of all phenomena in the universe. The historical approach to texts has a uniquely valuable place in liberal education, complemented by the equally powerful disciplines of mind to be found in mathematics, science, and the arts, including literature. These are the core disciplines of a liberal education. They seek not to alter individual behavior or social interaction as such; if such changes do occur, it is only as a by-product of intellectual development, not its central purpose. They do seek to develop the individual's capacity to cope with the biggest of all human questions and to contribute his mite to the civil society. So although social behavior is not the primary goal of a liberal education, it is in fact one manifestation of a well-educated mind.

The problem before us, then, is whether we as a nation are genuinely interested in the intellectual development of all Americans. We have historically reserved such an education for the few in our exclusive private schools, in many fine parochial schools, and in those public schools where the children of the highly educated and the affluent congregate.

In the past, to neglect to provide a powerful education for all Americans was not only acceptable, but desirable, since mind-numbing lifework in the factory, the mill, the farm, or the mine was thought to be more bearable for the workers if they were intellectually content with their lot. But such jobs are fast disappearing, being replaced by more sophisticated jobs requiring more thought, more analysis, more decision-making, and more understanding. Such an economy cannot provide jobs for the uneducated.

Rising Tides Raise All Boats

In our CHART experiments we have seen students blossom as they used their minds. We know that poor children and minority children are America's greatest untapped resource. We believe a powerful liberal education that seeks to develop their minds in every class and at every age from six to seventeen is the greatest single need in our public schools. Achieving such ends even with a few teachers in a few schools takes a tremendous effort, but it is an effort absolutely worth undertaking. What we have learned is that teachers and scholars need to work collaboratively so that new and developing knowledge in the disciplines can be available for teachers to use. Teachers need to think of their jobs as a life of continuous inquiry and study—and be rewarded for so thinking. They need to consider the classroom as an intersection among thinking adults, thinking students, and the texts that form the basis for thought. The texts in that classroom need to be valued by both students and the society, with teachers negotiating the selection of texts so as to meet the value criteria of both. The result of such a classroom would be a place where important work gets done by the students themselves.

Such a vision suggests that we value our children enough to abandon the pedagogy of poverty and work instead toward an intellectually rich education. Such an education would design the entire school not for social purposes primarily but for the intellectual development of all students. If forty-two minutes is not enough time to adequately study a text, then instead of cutting short the study when the bell rings for the social convenience of the school, we would turn off the bell for the intellectual convenience of the minds at work in the classroom. If the tests administered by the state place a high value on short, correct answers but the schoolroom places a high value on long, complex argument, then the state should reconsider the value of tests that ultimately honor social conformity rather than intellectual autonomy. If the teaching methods advocated by teacher preparation institutions emphasize social and psychological development at the expense of intellectual development, then they must seriously reconsider this balance in their classrooms. If text*books* offer little well-wrought language in favor of predigested conundrums, then they should be abandoned in favor of the authentic voices of the poets and scientists and historians who have constructed our culture and the cultures of others and whose idiosyncracies paradoxically speak for us all. And if we truly honor the minds of all of our children, we will encourage them all day and every day from first grade through twelfth to read and observe, to analyze and hypothesize, to answer back and to argue, and to create something new out of the voices of others so as to create a new set of voices to add to our culture.

In the pages that follow we offer the reader a look at some of the work we have in progress. The students, teachers, project directors, and researchers whose voices you will read have each tried to understand something about how reading, writing, and understanding culture should be done in the classroom. Teachers describe the processes they have set in motion, students their response to materials and ideas introduced in class, researchers the kind of thinking they see going on in the described classroom.

One of the most important features of a set of voices such as this is the sense one gets of dialogue—of trial and error—of collaboratively working through the problem of how to create rich discourse around some very human questions.

When teachers, students, artists, historians, parents, and others join forces to produce new understandings about the human condition, then powerful learning takes place in our schools. The learning is always provisional—a landmark in a lifelong journey school should assist every American to begin. We invite you to look at a few examples of people who have been thinking about how to get started.

Notes

1. Martin Haberman, "The Pedagogy of Poverty Versus Good Teaching." *Phi Delta Kappan* (December 1991): 290–94.

Some of the most positive results of the growing awareness of America's diverse cultures have been the opportunities for helping students discover real cross-cultural understanding. As a society we are going through a painful process of learning not just to get along, but also to respect one another and the differences between our cultures and heritages. It is an amazingly complicated process.

Students and schools are often caught in the middle of many competing forces. As Jai Richardson, a Los Angeles high school student says, "Everyone is telling us we have to get along, but no one is telling us how we're expected to live together, and we don't really understand each other. . . . We don't learn enough about our own culture, let alone about someone else's."

Many CHART projects work to encourage the understanding students such as Jai are struggling to find. There are no easy answers; there are no one-shot programs that will create tolerance and understanding, much less respect and appreciation; there is only a need to create new approaches to teaching about culture, to encouraging students to understand the origins and value of difference.

The three essays that follow describe different approaches to exploring cultural differences. They share an open-minded attempt to stimulate students' interest in some aspects of another culture unfamiliar to most students in the classes—Japanese culture in predominantly Hispanic, White, and African American classrooms in New York, Native American culture in largely Hispanic Los Angeles classrooms, and a variety of cultures in predominantly African American and Hispanic classroom in Miami. In each case the teachers then tie students' study of the "other" to the students' own lives, linking the learning to the students' personal sense of identity.

These essays represent three CHART projects that focus attention on specific cross-cultural issues. **New York and the World** links teachers with cultural institutions to create curricula and programs that will increase students' and teachers' appreciation of cultural diversity through interdisciplinary humanities. **HUMANITAS** strengthens humanities teaching in Los Angeles through teacher-developed, interdisciplinary, multicultural themes. **Inhabiting Other Lives** is designed to create a multicultural curriculum that will help overcome racial and ethnic barriers and conflicts among students.

Illustration by Jeremy Schnorr.

New York and the World
Kathleen Nilsen Fuentes and Philip Weinberg

We teach global humanities to ninth-graders at the High School of Telecommunication Arts and Technology in Brooklyn, New York. Its name notwithstanding, our school offers a general academic program. With almost 1,000 students enrolled, it is among the smallest high schools in the city. About 40 percent of the students are Hispanic, 35 percent White, 22 percent African American, and 4 percent Asian. Moreover, considerable diversity exists within each of these categories. An increasing proportion of our African American students, for instance, come from the non-Spanish-speaking Caribbean. The white population includes second- and third-generation Italians from nearby Bensonhurst, recent immigrants from the Arab world, as well as Irish- and Norwegian Americans from Bay Ridge. While five years ago the overwhelming majority of our Hispanic population was of Puerto Rican descent, Dominicans, Mexicans and other Central and South Americans now figure more prominently.

The wide range of cultural and economic circumstances of the student population poses certain challenges that are exacerbated by the endemic underfunding of urban schools. Many of these students arrive in ninth grade with deficient basic skills. Since teachers in our school, as in other New York City high schools, see upwards of 170 students every day (classes are "limited" to 34 students; teachers meet with five classes per day), the average student receives little individual attention.

While not a perfect solution, the New York and the World humanities program has helped us make school more meaningful in our students' lives. In this program we are able to engage students in meaningful humanities work during double class periods. These longer classes represent a departure from the traditional "factory" approach to education, wherein students receive instruction in discrete forty-minute units. When students spend two periods per day working with the same teachers and the same group of peers on related ideas, it is easier to develop an atmosphere of trust, in which students and teachers alike are willing to take risks that result in quality learning. In school, the student's world becomes smaller, less anonymous, more humane.

Kathleen Nilsen Fuentes teaches ninth- and tenth-grade Social Studies and Humanities at the High School of Telecommunication Arts and Technology in Brooklyn, New York. She holds a B.A. from the University of Toronto.

Philip Weinberg teaches ninth- through twelfth-grade English at the High School of Telecommunication Arts and Technology in Brooklyn, New York. He holds a B.A. from Swarthmore College and an M.A. from Teachers College at Columbia University.

Team Planning and Double Period Scheduling

A key component of the success of this program is that teachers plan together. Activities and lessons are designed to cross the traditional lines between disciplines and to help students connect different types of learning. The opportunity to use block programming and the school's general commitment to humanities allow teachers greater latitude in determining what happens in the classroom. Students are surprised; there is a lot of relearning for them. They constantly protest, "But this isn't social studies" or "You're supposed to be an English teacher." By the end of the term, these accusations have become compliments.

Students who feel accountable to two teachers often complete readings, projects, and other assignments more diligently. Much of our common planning time is spent discussing individual students' progress. With two teachers monitoring their work, it isn't as easy for the students to squirm out of obligations. Initially, students are somewhat taken aback when we display our awareness of their performance in the "other" class. "Why do you care about *that*—I'm doing your work, it's Ms. Nilsen's class I'm failing" is a typical response. Gradually, students stop trying to shirk their responsibilities and begin to develop their own internal sense of accountability.

The Development of the Humanities Program

Our humanities course began to take shape three years ago. Under the auspices of the New York and the World program, we attended staff development workshops in preparation to write and implement a global humanities curriculum. New York State social studies teachers are mandated to teach about the Middle East, Africa, Latin America, Asia (South and Southeast Asia, China, Japan), the Soviet Union, Eastern Europe, and Western Europe in the ninth- and tenth-grade years. Embracing that mandate, the New York and the World program solicited proposals from New York City high schools interested in taking an integrated humanities approach to global studies, rather than continuing the standard instruction by discipline.

During 1988–89, the first full year of its implementation, the New York and the World program focused mainly on course content. This made sense, since lack of expertise is what prevents some of us from teaching about non-Western cultures. In terms of curriculum design, the real breakthrough occurred for us that summer. The New York and the World program sponsored a five-day retreat where we met in teams to translate what we had learned about Asia into a curriculum with scope and sequence. This scope and sequence outlined what we intended to cover, and how we would go about presenting this material to students.

What a luxury for teachers to be able to talk and plan, away from the day-to-day pressures of school! The Asia unit was to span the entire second semester, and would build upon the work we had done with Africa, the Middle East, and Latin America. During the fall term we would emphasize the theme of identity as a function of culture. For the spring term and our study of Asia, we decided to focus on group versus individual identity. *Romeo and Juliet* and James Baldwin's story "Sonny's Blues" bridge the two terms. Both texts invite discussion of the effects of groups on individual identity, as well as the relative weight of group and individual identity in different societies throughout history. We return to these texts again and again during our study of India's caste system, arranged marriages, Confucianism, communism versus free enterprise, and Japan's group-oriented culture.

In global studies, human constants that cross cultures tend to be emphasized. Rites of passage associated with puberty (of special interest to fourteen- to sixteen-year-olds!), family groupings, religious explanations of death and the afterlife all fall into this category of "human constants." In the case of Asia, we departed somewhat from our usual approach. It was a general sense of East and West, a feel for similarities as well as differences between Eastern and Western cultures that would be part of a more privileged adolescent's cultural vocabulary, that we set out to inculcate in the course of the Asia unit.

We are fortunate to have the Metropolitan Museum of Art just a subway ride away, and during the time we were teaching this unit, funding was still available for one trip per semester. Kathleen had done a summer institute at the Met on Japanese art, so we decided to make that collection the focus of our museum visit, which would culminate in a more general study of Japanese art and aesthetics.

Our students had a more immediate and comfortable response to visual information than to complex written texts. Though the students might not have been likely to be familiar with the art, or with the cultural values that characterize East and West, we hoped that this approach would both catch their attention and provide a concrete example of the values we would encounter when we read a Japanese novel during the course of the unit.

In teaching the arts of unfamiliar cultures, we try to strike a balance between applying a universal aesthetic and respecting a culturally-specific aesthetic. Both of us feel strongly that we do not want to use non-Western literature or other art as mere "artifacts" for the study of culture. Such "anthropologizing" of art, in our view, is both patronizing and reductive. Aesthetics transcends culture, at a level of experience we consider valuable for our students. At a certain point in experiencing the art directly, our students almost internalize the nature of a Japanese response. Through this aesthetic response, they reach a different level of understanding, one where similarities are more important than differences. Nonetheless, though intrinsic to human nature, an aesthetic sensibility also needs to be cultivated.

To introduce the principles of Japanese aesthetics, we use selections from a lecture on the subject by Donald Keene in which he draws heavily on Kenko's seventeenth-century *Essays on Idleness*, and Yukio Mishima's novel *The Sound of Waves*. Keene identifies and expounds upon four aspects of Japanese aesthetics: suggestion, irregularity, simplicity, and perishability. In class, students are divided into groups and assigned one of these characteristics. For the next day's class, they must explain this characteristic using two examples drawn from *The Sound of Waves*. Finally, each group presents two objects found in their own lives that, in their view, embody the characteristic they have been assigned.

About the Japanese predilection for the ephemeral, or that which perishes, Keene writes:

> Signs of wear and tear such as the fraying of a silk wrapper . . . would be likely to dismay most other people . . . but in Japan an object of such perfection, of such gleaming newness that it might have been made yesterday has seemed less desirable than a work that has passed through many hands and shows it.[1]

Students cite and explain Japanese examples provided by Keene: a cup whose cracks have been mended with gold, a worn scroll. One group displayed a frayed and patched pair of jeans, which triggered a discussion of consumer trends and of how worn-looking jeans often cost more than new ones. With few exceptions, we agreed that there was something especially alluring about worn jeans, though there was some dispute about whether that special worn quality was something that could be purchased off the rack. Another student showed us a school bag that she (and older siblings before her) had used for primary school in her native Colombia. A wooden subway booth counter, eroded by years of hands scooping out their tokens, was described but, thankfully, not brought in. To illustrate asymmetry, part of Keene's concept of irregularity, one group invited in a schoolmate with a particularly striking asymmetrical haircut.

Students continued to look for images that correspond to these four principles as they read Mishima's *The Sound of Waves*. Early in this novel of life in a small fishing village, Shinji, the novel's main character, tends to the day's catch.

> Shinji took them off the hooks with his bare hands. The flatheads fell to the blood-smeared deck, their white bellies gleaming. The black, wet bodies of the soles, their little eyes sunk deep in folds of wrinkles, reflected the blue of the sky.[2]

Where feasible, the principles of Japanese aesthetics are used as a frame of reference for such descriptions. While one has to wonder whether Kenko had the stench of dead fish in mind when he described the Japanese affinity for that which perishes, the parallel does not escape our students. The fact that the students' applications of these principles would not stand up to scholarly analysis does not faze us. Through such playful application of the aesthetic principles, we know from experience that the casual facility with Japanese aesthetics we are trying to cultivate will creep into our students' thinking. After all this, in final preparation for the museum visit, students are given a conventional quiz that measures their ability to identify and apply the concepts.

The museum visit is designed with numerous objectives in mind. In the American Wing, students select their favorite works and share their choices with partners. This guided activity pushes students to explore their own sense of American aesthetics and prepares them visually for the comparison with Japanese. A short jaunt up a back staircase takes them into the Sackler Galleries of Japanese Art. In the Japanese galleries, the students apply what they learned in class about Japanese aesthetics. By the end, most students have internalized enough about Japanese aesthetics that they unself-consciously incorporate a "Japanese" sensibility into their "personal" reactions to the art.

By ninth grade, our students are conversant with the principles of traditional Western aesthetics. With virtually no prompting, they walk into the American Wing of the Metropolitan Museum of Art and select their favorites based on color, attractiveness of subject, verisimilitude, expression of American values. One student chose Gilbert

Stuart's *Matilda Stoughton de Jaudenes* "because of the great use of colors" and "very neat details." "The painting," she goes on to write, "looks so realistic it appears as a photograph." Along similar lines, a student selects Matthew Pratt's *The American School* because "it looked so real, the way Pratt drew the people." Another student, regarding her selection of Frederic Church's *Heart of the Andes*, focused first on the "colors and shapes of the mountains," then went on to describe "the size of the land and the freedom of the mountains." In her view, the painting depicted "the cheering and mysterious sight of the earth, the accomplishments of nature and adaptation of humans to nature . . . [and] the facts of life and freedom."

From the American Wing we proceed to the Sackler Galleries of Japanese Art. The space itself has an utterly different feel: hushed rather than resonant, dimly lit, not expansive like the American Wing but low and contained. This quiet moment lends itself to a large group encounter with a Buddhist altar, then with a Shigarake ware storage jar from the Muromachi period. Students take pride in their ability to recognize the worn, unrestored quality of the Buddha, or the irregular surface of the storage jar. We prod them in certain directions, fill in historical details where appropriate, and generally model the process of looking at art.

The students are then set loose to complete their activity sheet in the company of a partner. We circulate, helping students who have trouble applying the concepts, pressing more accomplished students to observe harder. As students move freely about the galleries, larger groups form around certain displays, then disband as they discover other works.

Empowered with their new vocabulary and secure in their own responses, students engage with the art in ways that never fail to surpass our expectations. One student defends the storage jar against the allegation that "this is not art and does not deserve to be in a museum." Having made pots herself, she draws her audience's attention to the visible coils, which, according to her, suggest the hand of the farmer-craftsman who fashioned it back in the fifteenth century. One of us draws the students' attention to the designs created by the ash in the firing, and we exchange ideas about what figures are suggested by these shapes. One student sees a map of the United States, and the others agree that irregular glazing of one area indeed recalls that familiar outline. The question of whether a Japanese viewer would likely see the same map is posed. No, they think not. Some students search in vain for something that resembles a map of Japan. Left alone, assuming they are out of the teachers' earshot, students discover a truly impressive variety of forms on the jar's surface, most of which would have to be censored from this essay.

Another group of students is admiring a Shoin room. We share our marvel at how all the elements of Japanese aesthetics studied in class can be seen in this one space: the use of perishable materials, such as the paper that covers the sliding doors or the straw tatami mats; the room's uncluttered simplicity; the asymmetry of the *tokonoma* (alcove); the branch painted on the hanging scroll, which is not realistic like the American paintings we just saw but monochromatic and suggestive. We think about whether we would want to live in such a place, and the consensus is not surprising, considering the clutter and chaos of our urban environment. The students use words like "private," "quietlike," "closed," "secure," and "harmony" to describe their feelings about the room.

The Met rotates its displays, and this particular year a six-panel screen depicting the four seasons particularly captivated many of the students. While the screen is monotone and sparse, one student wrote that "the landscape looks alive and flowing with vegetation." He referred to "people walking through mountains and crossing rivers, nothing complicated, all straightforward and simple. . . . For the people who saw the painting," he concluded, "it would always be there in their thoughts and memory." In the galleries, one of us asked some students how a four seasons theme might be rendered by an American artist. A sometimes volatile young woman, after momentary reflection, blurted out: "The colors would make it too obvious." It sounded like an accusation! After that, we marveled anew at the Japanese artist's ability to depict the seasons *without* using color as a visual cue.

One thing our students probably do have in common with their teenage peers from around the country is their fascination with implements of aggression and war. Highly ornamented samurai swords do not fit neatly into our game plan (simplicity, suggestion, etc.), and some student inevitably notices this inconsistency. The teacher can try to suppress discussion of swords and armor (futile—we tried that the first time around!), or use this example to emphasize how neat academic generalizations seldom capture the complex realities of a culture. We opt not to ignore, this time, the objects in the galleries that hold the greatest interest for them. Once they have had their fill of the warriors' accoutrements, students are challenged to find other exceptions to the "rules" we learned. Alas, the galleries offer an array of examples: intricately embroidered kimonos, the patterned borders of hanging scrolls, ornate lacquerwork. Upon scrutiny, for one group of students, the very concept of "simplicity" turned out to be more complex than we had expected. A visually perceptive young woman posited that even though the overall effect of Japanese brush painting was one of simplicity to an American viewer, Japanese artists paint with "so many different kinds of lines—thick, thin, straight, and curved" that the lines have a complexity of their own. This phase of the visit was recalled a couple of weeks later, as we read an excerpt from "We, Japanese" that described Japanese corporate culture. One student challenged the implication that *all* Japanese are group-oriented team players. To defend her position, she recalled how "Mr. Weinberg and Ms. Nilsen told us that all Japan art was simplicity." An unexpected application of Japanese aesthetics to the study of culture!

To design the writing assignment, we went back to our original objective of East versus West. During the course of the year, as they study works of fiction, the students do "point of view" writing. The student imagines he or she is a Palestinian teenager; Jomo Kenyatta; a participant in Gandhi's Salt March; Juliet's best friend; etc. The student then writes about a particular situation from that character's point of view. The main character from *The Sound of Waves*, the text they read in English, is Shinji the young fisherman. In the novel, he falls in love with Hatsue, daughter of a prosperous village shipowner. We hoped the use of the point of view would demonstrate the student's ability to see American art through Japanese eyes and react to the art of Japan as if a member of that culture. Students able to do that, we felt, would have mastered the material to our satisfaction. Besides, knowing that even our most reluctant pupils enjoy assuming the identity of other teenagers—especially when they are in love!—we are not above pandering to their tastes to ensure the assignment is done.

The assignment the students received read as follows:

> Imagine you are either Hatsue or Shinji from *The Sound of Waves*. You are visiting Brooklyn, staying with the family of a student at this school. Today you went on a class trip to the Metropolitan Museum of Art to view both Japanese and American art.
>
> Write a letter to your friend (Hatsue or Shinji) back in your village. Compare the Japanese and American art that you saw at the museum. Which American works did you like? Why? Which Japanese works did you like? Why? In general, how does the American art compare to the Japanese art with which you are accustomed? How did the American students respond to the Japanese art? How did you feel about their responses?
>
> In addition to discussing the art you saw, you will certainly want to share with your friend some of the experiences you have had with the American students. How does life in New York compare with life on Uta Jima?
>
> This letter should demonstrate your understanding of American and Japanese art, your familiarity with *The Sound of Waves*, and your general sense of similarities and differences between Japanese and U.S. culture.

Quite frankly, the letters were not the neat synopses of Japanese and American aesthetics we had, as pedagogues, naively hoped they would be. Students are expert at resisting teachers' attempts to impose an agenda. Some of them, to our dismay, mentioned the art only in passing, before getting down to the more vital matter of how life in New York City compared to life in the fishing village, and how much they pined for their lovers. The others addressed the art to varying degrees, almost all with a surprising degree of competence. What we did not receive, it should be noted, were contrived applications of everything they had learned about Japanese aesthetics to the art they saw in the museum. Almost without exception, the art entered the letters in a natural way.

The student sample included here, by Susanna, both documents the strengths of our approach and raises questions about how our student population, given the challenges outlined at the outset of this article, should be taught. Susanna, it is clear from the text, felt a natural affinity for the art. The "point of view" worked for Susanna: she creates a believable Hatsue, and through Hatsue's eyes demonstrates a Japanese sensibility.

As a writer, thinker, and person, Susanna is typical of students who blossom in a humanities program such as ours. Highly motivated, she arrives at seven o'clock every morning, takes advantage of the school breakfast program, then usually comes to one of our classrooms to chat and complete homework assignments. Born in Puebla, Mexico, Susanna had lived in this country for only five years, so reading and writing in the English language was still a struggle for her. The technical deficiencies of her writing, however, do not impede her from delving into a point of view assignment or grappling with aesthetics and culture.

A more traditional approach to English or social studies, in which the textbook serves as the only source of information and mastery must be demonstrated exclusively through multiple choice exams and formal expository writing, might shut students like Susanna out of the learning process. Through the kinds of projects and activities outlined here, Susanna and others like her are motivated to shine in areas where they feel some innate competence. Once the study of the humanities hooks students like Susanna on thinking and learning, we believe the more traditionally valued skills of formal writing and taking multiple choice exams will follow. While the specific impact of humanities on our students is not easy to pinpoint, the strides they have made since the program's inception seem to lend validity to our convictions and approach.

Notes

1. "Japanese Aesthetics" is taken from "The Pleasures of Japanese Literature," a lecture by Donald Keene, delivered at the Metropolitan Museum of Art in New York City.

2. Yukio Mishima, *The Sound of Waves*, translated by Meredith Weatherby (New York: Alfred A. Knopf, 1956).

Acknowledgements

We would like to thank our students, in particular Jesus Cordero, Anna Soysal, Lizette Zurita, as well as Susanna Sosa: their enthusiasm and insights are truly our source of inspiration. In addition, our thanks go to supervisors Larry Abrams and Ellen Victor, whose support on many fronts has made the global humanities program a reality.

Letter to Shinji
Susanna Sosa

Hello: Shinji

I'm writing you this letter hoping you are fine. My love, a few days ago I had a class in both American and Japanese art. I know what you are thinking right now. You're probably thinking that I like to compare things of Japan. I really can't deny it because I know it is true.

When I saw the American art I was amazed. I noticed that American art is different from Japan. The art was very colorful and very creative. Of all the portraits I saw I didn't see any lines as in the portraits of Japan. Americans paint things the way they see it. On the other hand, the Japanese paint with distinct lines. In addition, most of them paint objects of how they feel about that particular object.

"The Flower Girl" was the American painting I liked the most. The reason I liked it was because it was very colorful which it attracted my attention. The second reason, I liked it was because Amelia had a bouquet of flowers on her hand. In addition, I liked a Japanese portrait named Torri Liyoman. I liked it because it had distinct lines. For instance, thin, thick, straight, and curved ones. I also, liked this portrait because it gave attention to people.

To be honest with you the painting that I am more accustomed to is the Japanese painting simply because Japanese paint of how they think or feel about that particular thing. Rather than that, the Americans paint exactly the way they see it. In which I guess is more complicated.

The American students were surprised when they saw the Japanese art because the color was mostly black and white. Some of them told me that they never thought they will see a lot of lines on the portraits. When I heard the comments I was surprised because I never thought they will respond that way.

In our village we love to go fishing. Even you pray to God, to become a great fisher. Now don't deny it. Well, anyway in New York they find fishing boring. What a big difference??

Write soon!!!

Love Hatsue

Origins
Marie Collins

California is the nation's most racially diverse state, with a greater percentage of Asian and Latino residents than any other state and the second-highest number of blacks and American Indians of any state, census figures show.

Los Angeles Times, *June 13, 1991*

The challenge to educators which diversity [within the student population] presents is even more compelling in the Los Angeles Unified School District where eighty-six percent of the students are 'minority,' one in five students lives in poverty, and about a third are not proficient in English.

Los Angeles Times, *November 8, 1991*

In an article titled "Little Progress Made with Classroom Racial Tensions" (*Los Angeles Times*, September 21, 1992), Stephanie Chavez describes an angry clash between Asian and African-American students in a Los Angeles high-school algebra class. The flare-up ignited when an African-American student's "question was not promptly answered. . . . Angry words and racial epithets rang out from both sides of the divide"; and although violence was averted, "algebra class would never be the same." We might ask, How did these students and their teacher get to the brink of violence in their daily struggle to learn algebraic formulas? But perhaps the more appropriate question is why the incident didn't occur before it did, given the classroom climate Chavez describes: "Tensions had been brewing . . . all year. Asian students took seats on one side of the room, blacks on the other." Added to this self-imposed segregation was the complaint by African-American students that "the Asian teacher paid more attention to high achievers, many of the Asians."

This kind of scene has become all too familiar, for we live in a time when "schoolyards are rife with racial tension and students have witnessed an explosion of civil unrest that

Marie Collins teaches advanced placement English and eleventh-grade American Studies at San Pedro High School in the Los Angeles Unified School District. She holds a B.A. from Hofstra University, an M.A. from California State University at Dominguez Hills, and is currently a Ph.D. candidate at the Claremont Graduate School. She is the author of "Fostering Analytical Thinking and Writing in High School," which appeared in *Teaching Analytical Writing* (UCLA Publishing, 1988) and "Variations on the American Dream," published in *The City and Literature* (Rutgers University Press, 1982). She has a keen interest in global education and in multicultural literature. Ms. Collins is on leave during the 1992–93 school year to work as an American Council of Learned Societies Fellow at the University of California-Los Angeles.

their textbooks have not yet recorded. . . . " Still, "racial issues are often deemed too complex, too potentially volatile for education to address in the classroom." Yet, if we educators have learned anything from the Los Angeles riots in April 1992, it is that this issue cannot remain what Kenyon Chan, a psychologist specializing in racism, calls "the forgotten subject." The imperative to act is articulated by Jai Richardson, a senior at Dorsey High School in Southwest Los Angeles when he says, "Everyone is telling us we have to get along, but no one is telling us how we're expected to live together, and we don't really understand each other. . . . We don't learn enough about our own culture, let alone about someone else's."

It is a commitment to multicultural education—an approach that seeks to develop in all students an understanding and respect for the diverse cultures that represent American life—that guides the HUMANITAS program at San Pedro High School. What our American Studies team has attempted to do is to create a humanities curriculum that provides diverse perspectives. Reynaldo F. Macias, a specialist in multicultural education, maintains that "we know that a lot of what is going on in the classroom is harmful to the development of . . . understanding across racial, social, and cultural lines. . . . Yet we are not doing enough to change it. . . . " We hope our interdisciplinary, humanities-based approach is one way of responding to this challenge to change.

HUMANITAS is a model program that was initiated in the Los Angeles Unified School District in 1986 by the Los Angeles Educational Partnership (LAEP). The HUMANITAS program provides support and guidance to teams of teachers collaborating on the development of interdisciplinary, thematic, writing-based humanities curricula. At San Pedro High School, we have developed a multicultural American Studies course for more than one hundred students that combines American literature, composition, U.S. history, art, and philosophy. The course is open to any eleventh-grade student; it is not an "honors" course and there are no grade requirements for admission—students simply bring a desire to learn the "humanities way." The students in recent HUMANITAS groups have ranged from gifted to remedial, approximately ten percent of whom have been considered Limited English Proficient.

The course is taught by a team of teachers: my colleagues are Nick Zorotovic (U.S. History) and John Calise (Humanities/English). While we are each associated with a particular discipline, we all teach humanities—which means we constantly cross over often arbitrary discipline lines. One of the first units we teach is an eight-week unit called Origins. As the literature teacher on the team, it is my task to provide a basis for students to understand the spiritual resources of minority peoples through an in-depth study of representative literature. The interdisciplinary character of our program also allows students to examine the historical, social, and cultural forces that influence writers and shape their unique contributions to American literature.

Origins focuses on three questions. The primary question is, Who am I? Part of the students' time during the unit is spent researching their own ethnic origins. Each student completes an original coat of arms, a family tree, and an oral history taken from an older relative. The students' self-discovery can be very positive; they genuinely enjoy learning the meaning of their names or finding out about some almost forgotten family tradition. Students' enthusiasm for researching names or recording oral histories from family members transfers to other areas of their learning in very important ways: (1) they become aware that the most valuable learning arises from a genuine "need to know"; (2) they come to see themselves as "active agents" in their own learning; (3) they begin to value their own intelligence and their own unique experiences; (4) they begin to use research skills—especially "primary sources"; and (5) they find new motivation for learning when they are offered choices and are engaged—they do their best work and their success tends to be repeated in other situations.

One year a parent came in to work with our students (both male and female) on a quilt in which each square symbolized a student's ethnic heritage or some aspect of family history. One of my students put it this way in her evaluation: "I am amazed at how close I am to an enriched culture [Mexican] and yet how ignorant I am. . . . I am a bit like Arturo Islas [author of a novel about Mexican Americans, *The Rain God*] wanting to let others know us. . . . "

The second question students consider is, Who are you? Students read literary works that capture the experience of Native Americans, European immigrants, African Americans, Mexican Americans, and peoples of the Asian Pacific Rim. The readings include well-known works as well as those of lesser-known men and women who reflect the makeup of the American cultural tradition. There is a concerted effort to present students with literature not typically anthologized and by so doing to expand the traditional "canon" of American literature. Participation in a number of National Endowment for the Humanities summer institutes has broadened my knowledge of multicultural literature, and I have been able to develop curriculum around some of these works, including Rudolfo Anaya's *Bless Me, Ultima*, Paule Marshall's *Praisesong for the Widow*, Arturo Islas's *The Rain God*, and *The Woman Warrior* by Maxine Hong Kingston.

Third, we consider the question, Who are we? After studying various groups of people, students must synthesize their knowledge. We ask them to answer the question posed by Jean de Crèvecoeur in 1782 in *Letters from an American Farmer*: "What then is the American . . . ?"

As a final exam, students are asked to form cooperative groups and create a metaphor that captures the essence of the Origins unit and that answers the three questions we had considered. This project not only tests what they have learned and how well they understand this knowledge, but it also requires students learn to work together. One group of students constructed a three-foot-high cardboard monolith as their project. Each side consisted of a montage, combining elements from different ethnic groups we had studied, including those of the students in the group. Distinct images were blended artistically to produce an undifferentiated, harmonious creation.

Using Literature

For the purposes of this essay, I will focus on the second part of the Origins unit, which involves literature. The core novel all of our students study during the unit is Hal Borland's *When the Legends Die*. While it may not be the quintessential work on the Native American experience, it is an engaging piece of fiction for students of average reading ability. Another important fact is that the novel is on the district's "approved" reading list and so may be purchased with textbook funds.

We begin our study with indigenous people for several reasons. On the most general level, the Native American worldview, cultural values, and oral tradition provide a rich contrast to the Western cultural tradition. In addition, we can bring into the discussion information about prehistory and the Native American ancestors who came from Asia to this continent thousands of years ago.

The novel, set in southwestern Colorado in the early part of the century, tells the story of a Ute Indian named Thomas Black Bull. Bull experiences alienation when he finds that the "old ways" of his tribe clash with the "new ways" he is forced to adopt in a white man's world. Only when he returns to the mountains of his ancestors does he find peace and harmony with his surroundings, and only then is he able to accept and affirm his own identity. Later on in the unit, students see this tension arise again in the literature of other ethnic groups who must decide how much to sacrifice in order to assimilate into the majority culture.

My approach to teaching this novel involved interdisciplinary activities to create context (ways *into* the novel), understanding (ways *through* the novel) and finally a chance to apply their learning in a creative project (ways *beyond* the novel).

> It had been a long journey, he thought, the long and lonely journey a man must make when he is lost and searching for himself, particularly one who denies his own past, refuses to face his own identity. There was no question now of who he was. The All-Mother's words, in the vision, stated it beyond denial: "He is my son." He was a Ute, an Indian, a man of his own beginnings, and nothing would ever change that. He had tried to change it. . . . And still he had to find the way back to himself, to learn . . . the simple truth . . . the ties that bind a man to the truth of his own being, his small part of the enduring roundness.[1]

Ways INTO the Novel

Our exploration of the novel builds upon the curriculum of previous years. For example, "Myths and Legends" is a theme covered in the ninth grade; *Medea* is read in the tenth grade. With this prior experience, when we look at the myths of Native American peoples students can and do draw parallels. To strengthen this knowledge, we also spend several days discussing what anthropology can tell us about indigenous peoples. Often we continue the study of myths and legends by having students write a legend or family story they recall being told as a child. Discussion follows and students notice the similarities among their stories. For example, Hispanic students are usually familiar with some version of the Legend of La Llorona, the wailing woman who murders her children and then throws them in a lake to spare them a worse fate. Students familiar with Greek mythology see the parallels between her story and the myth of Medea. In class discussion students also consider the purpose of legends: what worldview or cultural values do they represent?

Another activity gives the students the opportunity to read several tales from the Inuit, again trying to identify the values that the stories impart. While we strive to help students learn to be analytical, we don't try to arrive at an "authoritative" explanation for why certain stories were told in the way they were. We simply want students to focus on certain patterns, repeated images, or recurring themes in the tales and then suggest some possible values that the stories impart. As a teacher I draw on authorities such as Paula Gunn Allen, who writes:

> The experience and the traditions of American Indians are complex and diverse rather than simple and unitary. . . . But the ritual life of the tribes, the "religion" of the tribes is also a common factor. For although our traditions are as diverse as the tribes who practice and live within them, they are all earth-based and wilderness-centered; all are "animistic," polytheistic, concerned with sacred or nonpolitical power, and all incorporate patterns that many in the western world identify as profane.[2]

At this point, students are given copies of *When the Legends Die*. I ask them to read the epigraph and to consider its importance as they read the novel. "When the legends die, the dreams end," writes Borland. "When the dream ends, there is no more greatness."

Students are also asked to consider this quote from Leslie Marmon Silko's novel *Ceremony*, which suggests why we tell stories.

> Distances and days existed in themselves then; they all had a story. They were not barriers. If a person wanted to get to the moon, there was a way; it all depended on whether you knew the directions—exactly which way to go and what to do to get there; it depended on whether you knew the story of how others before you had gone.[3]

At this point, the students have gathered "stories" from their own family members. They understand that these stories are a way to keep alive the experiences of a group and also to point the way for future generations to follow—stories shape one's reality and personal and cultural identity.

Using Visual Material

I often use art as a means of engaging students in their learning. After viewing slides of Native American artwork, groups of students illustrate an account of the beginning of the world—and like early peoples they may use only pictures, not words. Each group's drawing is then shared with the entire class. Through this activity, students learn the power of symbols to communicate.

Next, we look at a transparency I've drawn of the *Walam Olum*, the Delaware tribe's account of natural phenomena expressed in pictographs painted on stone.[4] We go through the story and try to infer from it some of the tribe's ideals and values. With help, the students can see, for example, that the Delaware valued knowledge and leisure; that generosity and peace among people was considered important; and that by contrast, evil was anything that produced discord. I make a point of telling students that to this day members of the tribe recite this story in select ceremonies in order to keep their heritage alive.

In the same way, I use a transparency of Paul Revere's engraving of Philip (Metacomet), American Wampanoag Indian Chief. The work, done a century after "King

Philip" led the final Indian resistance against the Massachusetts colonists, reveals the artist's sympathetic attitude toward the Indian culture, overpowered by the European settlers with their more advanced methods of warfare and trade.

Ways THROUGH the Novel

HUMANITAS is a writing-based humanities curriculum, and so we try to provide many and varied writing experiences for our students. One of the activities that fosters critical thinking and analytical writing about literature is the "Reading Log," a simple two-column journal format in which students note passages that they find particularly powerful or interesting in one column, and their responses to or observations about these passages in the second column. A large body of convincing research documents the value of students' personal responses to their reading.[5] We try to design writing assignments that will draw on this research.

We try to connect students' writing to their own lives and experiences, the reading assignments, and current events. As an example, in 1991 the solar eclipse provided an excellent opportunity for a creative writing assignment during the reading of *When the Legends Die*:

> ASSIGNMENT: On July 11, 1991, at about 11:27 AM, there was an eclipse of the sun—an event that will not happen again until the year 2017 (when most of you will be middle-aged like me!)
>
> We have the benefit of modern scientific information to explain seven minutes when the earth "went dark"; but try to imagine how this same event might have been viewed by American Indians thousands of years ago. From what you have learned about their culture and worldview, write an account from an Indian's point of view about "The Day the Sun Went Away."

The following are excerpts from students' writing.

> Today is the day our Father the Earth and his Brother the Moon did battle over the heavens. Our ancestors have seen this battling going on for years; and every time the brothers fight, the Sun defeats the Moon. Although the Sun is the stronger brother, he is courteous enough to share the heavens with the Moon even after their fierce battles. The Great Spirit shows us his disapproval of fighting by making the sky grow dark.
>
> Jose

(A tribe's Elder speaks to the children.)

My sons, we have seen the world darken for a short time, but you must not be frightened. The Great Spirit has given us a test of faith. We can not abandon faith in the spirit, just as he will never abandon his people. We have taken care of Our Mother the Earth and now Our Father the Sky will take care of us if we are brave and trust in the Spirit who loves us.

Jorge

(A mother explains the eclipse to her child.)

My son, the Sun went away because the spirits of the sky are having a gathering just like the tribe's gatherings when we talk about ways to protect and shelter ourselves. Today the Sun asks the spirits how they can protect and preserve the Earth so that it will remain a beautiful and safe home for you as you grow up. This event happens rarely; so when it is to come again, you must pray to the spirits of the sky letting them know you are caring for the earth.

Laura

Because theirs is a predominantly oral tradition, Native Americans often recite songs and chants as part of their rituals. Students work together to write simple songs (poems) in a variety of forms:

Haiku

A new sun stretches,
Its warmth and music bringing
A clear, crisp morning.

Ways BEYOND the Novel

Once students have completed their reading of the novel and have explored various aspects of the Native American experience through other readings,[6] writing, and discussion they are given "extension" activities like the following:

Read the article "The Question of Reparations for American Indians" (*Los Angeles Times*, August 7, 1988) and prepare a debate on whether or not such reparations are appropriate in light of what you have learned during this unit.

All students complete a final project inspired by their study of *When the Legends Die*. The complete assignment follows this essay. Briefly, students are asked to:

1. Create names for themselves that reflect a significant or important aspect of their lives.
2. Write a series of songs to fit the incidents in the novel, expressing intense feeling and using vivid description and rhythm.
3. Write an account of an actual or imagined personal vision quest.

4. Create a cover design appropriate to the symbols and subject explored in the items above.

This culminating assignment—which results in students creating metaphors that capture what they have learned throughout the unit—was one type of assessment we used. The projects, the record of group process involved, and any writing went into the students' portfolios. The students were then able to go back to these portfolios during subsequent units to revise, add to, or subtract from their work as they acquired new insights and new learning.

The following samples of the writing by an "average" student attests to the success of this project.

<u>Name</u>

The name that I chose is "El Savrin" (which means like a wise person). When I was just a little child in Peru, my Dad tried to prepare me for school. He would teach me math, science, and many other things that I did not know about. My brothers tell me that every evening he would explain how he wanted me to be successful in school and in my life.

I learned more and more at home from my father, until I was old enough for school. Everything in class seemed to be easy for me. . . . All my teachers wrote happy faces on my tests, quizzes, and class work. My Dad was so proud of me because I was successful at school and I was proud of him.

One day, we had an oral exam, and I was answering all of the questions. Then the teacher said, "Mario, from now on I will call you 'Savrin' because you always know everything." Soon my classmates started to call me "Savrin" too.

I laugh when my family tells me that story, because I know that I am not that "wise person" today. Still, I am trying to be!

<u>Vision Quest</u>

Sometimes I see visions related to my family and friends, but there is one vision in particular that I will never forget. This vision had to do with my grandfather—father of my father.

It all began at school almost two years ago. I was eating lunch with my friends when I felt a pain in the back of my head. This was strange because I never had a pain like that before. When I got home at 7:00 p.m., I felt tired and sleepy. So, I decided to go to bed. Once I started sleeping, I had a vision of a car accident in a place far away from the city. A place that I knew. I saw a car in flames and the Red Cross coming to take a person from the burning wreck. The terrible thing was that I saw my family and myself crying beside the side of the road.

I woke up crying and sweating, but there was nobody in my room. The next day, I tried to tell my mother about the dream, but she said she didn't have enough time to hear those things. Then I went to my grandparents house to tell them. I wanted to talk to my grandfather, but my grandmother told me that he wasn't there. He had gone to visit a friend's house far away from the city, and she was going to meet him at noon. As she spoke, the telephone kept ringing and ringing. She answered it and then began to scream. "What? An accident? I can't believe it!"

"Too late," I said. "Too late! It was my fault!"

Mario Sanchez

How to Measure Success?

The Center for the Study of Evaluation at the University of California-Los Angeles has provided evidence about the success of the HUMANITAS program.[7] Some significant results include the following:

• Students in the program wrote essays with better overall quality, more conceptual understanding of history, and more interdisciplinary references than comparison students.

• Traditionally low-achieving students made gains in essay quality equivalent to those of higher-achieving students.

• HUMANITAS students reported that the class had a strong positive effect on their overall academic achievement.

• HUMANITAS students reportedly felt more willing to work hard in class, enjoyed class more, and thought about their futures more than comparison students.

• Students learned to work well in groups and to gain academic self-confidence.

• HUMANITAS students were absent less often than comparison students.

• The school dropout rate was lower for HUMANITAS classes than for comparison-classes.

• Students reported that work in HUMANITAS classes was harder and that HUMANITAS teachers had higher expectations.

Still, if no data were available on the HUMANITAS program, we teachers would have all the evidence necessary to measure its success in terms of our students' demonstrated ability to reach their full potential in a learning climate of trust, tolerance, and mutual respect. In the *Origins* unit in particular, we are committed to the proposition that preparing our students to live and work together may be as important as teaching them to read and write. By all accounts, we have succeeded.

Notes

1. Hal Borland, *When the Legends Die* (New York: Harper & Row, 1963).

2. Paula Gunn Allen, *The Sacred Hoop* (Boston: Beacon Press, 1986), p. 78.

3. Leslie Marmon Silko, *Ceremony* (New York: Penquin Books, 1977).

4. The *Walam Olum* (the narrative, pictographs, and accompanying texts) are found in *American Indian Literature: An Anthology*, Alan R. Velie, ed. (Norman: University of Oklahoma Press, 1991), pp. 92–133.

5. The research alluded to is drawn from the "writing process" models and from the California Literature Project. In addition, HUMANITAS is working with a team of researchers from UCLA who are studying analytical writing. One statement of the principles that inform their work is "To the greatest extent possible, our instruction should help students find their own purposes and insights congruent with the expectations of our assignments, not box them into choices we've already predetermined." See *Teaching Analytic Writing*, George Gadda, Faye Peitzman, and William Walsh, eds. (Los Angeles: UCLA, 1988).

6. In addition to *When the Legends Die*, students read excerpts from *Ceremony* by Leslie Marmon Silko, *House Made of Dawn* by N. Scott Momaday, and *The Education of Little Tree* by Forrest Carter.

7. P. R. Aschbacher and J. L. Herman, *The HUMANITAS Program Evaluation Final Feport* (Los Angeles: UCLA Center for the Study of Evaluation, 1988, 1989).

HUMANITAS

Sample Instructions for the "Reading Log" for *When the Legends Die*

Directions: You will be keeping a "Reading Log" for each day's reading of the novel. The following are directions for this activity:

1. The entry each day should be about a page in length.
2. The entry may be personal and unpolished writing, i.e., you may want to comment on the characters or events, the language of a particular passage, or anything else that captures your interest (There is NO right or wrong!).
3. Credit will be given for completing an entry each day.
4. Entries, along with answers to study guide questions, will assist you in reviewing the entire novel.
5. Please note, these entries consist of your personal reactions to the reading; DO NOT SUMMARIZE THE PLOT!
6. The format consists of a two-column Log; the left side, column 1, will have the passage from the novel, and the right side, column 2, will have your reaction.
7. What will your Log "sound" like? In your entries, you may a) write how a passage makes you feel; b) explain why you chose the passage; c) argue with or speak to a character or to the author; d) write about what a passage reminds you of (in your own experience), etc.

HUMANITAS

Sample Instructions for the Creative Projects for *When the Legends Die*

Directions: In response to the novel, you are to complete three creative tasks as well as design a cover for your project. The following are the guidelines for the assignment:

I   NAMES—In chapter seven of Part I, Bessie tells her son, "You will soon know a name for yourself." When Tom meets a she-bear that is not afraid of him, he leaves part of his deer meat for her, and a bond develops between them. As a result of this experience, Tom knows he will call himself "Bear's Brother" from that point on.

When N. Scott Momaday, a famous Kiowa Indian and author of a book titled *The Names*, explains his fascination with names, he says, "I believe that an essential part of my reality, my being, consists in my name. If I had a name other than my own, I would be someone else." It was traditional for most Indians to "know" more than one name for themselves in the course of a lifetime. (In the same way we often have nicknames in addition to our given names.) Consider some of the names in the novel; note how descriptive they are—Frank No Deer, George Black Bull, Blue Elk, Luther Spotted Dog, etc.; now try to imagine how each of these characters came to know his name. What incident or personal characteristic made this name the appropriate one?

For this part of the project, you are to choose a name for yourself. Like Tom, your name should relate to some significant event or should reflect some important aspect of your life so far. Explain why you "know" this name is "an essential part of your reality, of your being." Describe the incident that occurred when you came to know your name.

II   SONGS—Songs (poems) and chants form an important part of Indian tradition since they convey their vision of the world and their spiritual life. As in the novel, songs were known for many different experiences—even though Tom and the other characters may not always have remembered the words; the songs were "as old as the [Ute] people." Some songs were "dream" or "vision" songs that were given by the Great Spirit and that could be heard only by the spirit. Others tell stories or form a part of a ritual dance or ceremony.

For the second part of your project, you are to write songs (poems) to fit the incidents in the novel, providing the words that seem appropriate. (See the "Language Worksheet" for the three topics and the two sample songs.) Be sure that your songs express intense feelings, have vivid descriptions and rhythm. *For extra credit*, you may write an additional song on any other topic of your choice.

HUMANITAS

Instructions for the Creative Projects for *When the Legends Die*

III VISION QUEST—In many tribes, young boys (and occasionally young girls) sought a vision by fasting and praying for four days and nights. N. Scott Momaday explains in his essay "A Vision Beyond Time and Place" what is meant by a vision. It was a "gift of seeing truly, with wonder and delight, into the natural world. . . . It is a matter of extrasensory as well as sensory perception. In addition to the eye, it involves the intelligence, the instinct, and the imagination. It is not only the perception of objects and forms but also of essences and ideals. . . ." During the quest for a vision, a nature spirit, such as the spirit of a tree, an animal, or a rainstorm would give the young person a song that conferred some special power. These traditional songs were not written down; instead they were chanted or sung, often to the rhythm of drums and gourd rattles.

For the last part of your project, you are to write an account of a vision quest of your own. You may invent all of the details about the experience or you may write about an experience you actually had when you gained a new insight into the meaning of life or the nature of human existence. Be sure to provide your reader with sufficient details about the quest and your new understanding.

IV COVER DESIGN—In addition to oral literature, Indian art provided another means of communicating ideas and beliefs. To unify all of the parts of your project, you are to design a cover that communicates your own ideas and beliefs. The following are some suggestions:

• A cover that depicts a key incident from the novel;
• A design that relates to your name or your account of the vision quest;
• A collection of symbols that are important in the novel;
• A "totem"— an animal or natural object that a tribe considered was related by blood (for example, the bear or the deer);
• Any other design you consider appropriate.

Inhabiting Other Lives
Carol Litman Green

Connections: Search for Beauty, Overcome Prejudice, and Inhabit Other Lives is a multicultural, multiethnic program in literature, writing, and human experience designed for use in high schools. The project was created by Dale Gary and me at Miami Norland Senior High School, and José Piedra, Haywood Randolph, and Joel Schackne at Miami Springs Senior High School, under the auspices of the Miami CHART project, Inhabiting Other Lives. This project works to empower and instruct teachers in the humanities in order to foster an appreciation for cultural and ethnic diversity, and to contribute to the reduction of prejudice.

Teacher participants in the Inhabiting Other Lives project participated in a four-week intensive summer institute at Florida International University. A team of coordinators from the Dade-Monroe Teacher Education Center—Karen Dreyfus, Joanne Kaspert, and Rosa Harvey—worked in conjunction with the Humanities faculty at FIU to provide a rich summer experience. We read and discussed works by authors from all over the world; we took field trips to Les Cousins, a Haitian bookstore, and the Cuban American Museum; and enjoyed Vinie Burrows's one-woman show *Walk Together Children* about the struggle of the African American woman, and Pearl Primus's inspirational dance interpretations. During our summer workshop we were offered a powerful invitation to inhabit other lives, and we did! Through our shared experience we learned about the role the humanities must play in multicultural education, we learned about our own unconscious prejudices and, most important, we learned about one another.

My own experiences as a teacher-learner have taught me that the most powerful and meaningful lessons are both emotional and intellectual. It was my desire to create lessons in which my students could respond both ways. In Connections my students read multicultural, multiethnic literature that reflects the themes of the project's title and participated in a cross-cultural pen pal exchange with students in another high school.

Our project connected two schools in the Dade County School System: Miami Norland Senior High School, composed predominantly of black students from Jamaica, the Bahamas, and the Caribbean Basin; and Miami Springs Senior High School, which serves predominantly Hispanic students from Cuba and Central America. For nine weeks, my tenth-grade honors English students at Miami Norland wrote letters to their

Carol Litman Green teaches ninth- and tenth-grade honors/gifted English and a philosophy colloquium for ninth- through twelfth-grade students at Miami Norland Senior High School. She received a B.A. in English from the University of Pittsburgh, an M.Ed. in Secondary Education from the University of Florida, and an Ed.S. equivalency in Gifted Education from Nova University. She is the coauthor of *Creating Connections: Building Community in the Secondary Classroom* (Dade Academy of Teaching Arts) and was recognized in 1988 as Peace Educator of the Year by the Grace Contrino Adams Peace Education Foundation.

ninth- to twelfth-grade pen pals at Miami Springs about their backgrounds, cultures, schools, and life experiences. All letters were sent through the school mail at no cost to the student or teacher. Students in the project were not allowed to share photos, telephone numbers, or home addresses, removing any element of risk and preventing students from judging pen pals on superficial characteristics. The "connection" was through writing alone. Throughout the project the students kept a "Connections Journal: A Journal of Self Discovery" to collect pen pal letters and their reactions to stories and novels, class discussions, and films.

Looking at Prejudice

Just before the students were to be paired with their pen pals, I began a three-week lesson on prejudice, stereotyping, and discrimination. Choosing appropriate materials for my students to study during this period was not a difficult task, since I was able to draw on both the ideas and materials of the summer institute as well as standard classroom resources that could be adapted for this lesson.

At the beginning of the pen pal project, I began by asking students to list their prejudices in their Connections Journal. I also asked them to analyze the basis of the prejudice. We discussed some of the items in the journals and concluded that prejudices are often emotional rather than rational, not limited to race, and are perpetuated by ignorance. The students also agreed that perhaps the most challenging and important element necessary to reducing prejudice is empathy—putting oneself in another's place, inhabiting other lives. One tenth-grade honors student, fourteen-year-old Kenric Leach, responded in his journal with the following poem:

Red, White, and Blue

Ever since we were all this high,
we've been taught to pledge allegiance
to the flag of the United States of America,
to a red, white, and blue which stands for
sacrifice, liberty, and justice,
the American way.

But that red, white, and blue meant something different
for my people.

To my people, red was the color
of the stripes on our backs after one of master's whippings,
and the blood which oiled the gears of the cotton industry.
It was the ground after a Mississippi lynching.
It was the fire in the eyes of a youth in Watts.
Now it's the color of a gangster's rag.

That's red to my people.

To my people, white was the color
of the master's face as he raped the black housemaid,
and the cotton which bent the backs of former kings and queens.
It was the hoods which covered faces and burned crosses in our yards.
It was the sign which hung over the *clean* water fountain.
Now it's the smiling that tells me to read lips.

That's white to my people.

To my people, blue was the color
of the heaven where our shackles would finally be loosened,
and of the uniform we wore when we fought for respect
at Gettysburg and Fort Wagner.
It was the color of the notes which wailed from a black man's
saxophone and created a style of music all our own.
Now it's the tears of a mother crying over her son,
slain in Bensonhurst.

That's blue to my people.

O, say does that star-spangled banner yet wave
o'er the land of the greed
and the home of the slave?

After reading this piece I was awed by Kenric's talent with words, ideas, and feelings. This poem is powerful on many levels. He sews the threads of the "flag of the United States of America," the flag that stands for sacrifice, liberty, and justice, with allusions to the history of African Americans in America. Although Kenric recounts the pain and violence of "master's whippings" and of the "raped black housemaid," he also voices pride for "the uniform we wore when we fought for respect at Gettysburg and Fort Wagner," and for "the notes which wailed from a black man's saxophone and created a style of music all our own." The poem ends dramatically, with a play on the words of our national anthem, and rhetorically asks if America is "the land of the greed and the home of the slave?" In a sense, this poem is a reflection of Kenric's view of the black man in American society. Although taught to respect the icons of white America, in reality the black man understands American symbols with a tragic sense of irony.

One of the most important objectives of the Connections project was to foster an appreciation for cultural diversity. Perhaps one of the first steps to appreciating cultural diversity is the acceptance and appreciation of one's own culture. This piece admirably demonstrates Kenric's pride in his heritage and an understanding of the duality of the black man's life in America. He certainly invites the reader to see the world through another's point of view.

In addition to their poetry and essays, students' journals kept me in tune with their frustrations, insights, and personal growth during the project. The journal was a good place for students to record feelings and ideas as well as a place for pre-reading and post-reading responses to sensitive questions.

Drawing on Literature

The next step in this lesson on prejudice was to introduce the literature. The two works I used were "Crackling Day," a story of racism in South Africa by Peter Abrahams, and "After You, My Dear Alphonse" a story about stereotyping and prejudice in America by Shirley Jackson. (Both stories were excerpted in the October 6, 1989, issue of *Scholastic Scope*.) Students first read "Crackling Day" and discussed how the characters responded to the racism each experienced. "After You, My Dear Alphonse" led to a discussion about where children learn prejudice. In a follow-up essay, students compared and contrasted the attitudes of prejudice and stereotyping by adults and by children in the two stories.

The students moved to the library to research the topic "The Legacy of Discrimination—Who Pays the Cost?" I guided the students' research through a series of questions designed to allow them to begin with personal opinions and later find support for their positions. The questions were as follows:

1. In your opinion, what types of discrimination exist in the United States today?
2. Are these types of discrimination being addressed by the United States? If so, how?
3. In your opinion, is there room for improvement in addressing the types of discrimination identified in your answer to question #1? If so, how?
4. Are there laws that protect against the types of discrimination listed in your answer to question #1? What are they?
5. Who suffers the most when discrimination is practiced, the victim or the perpetrator?
6. What active role can you play in helping to rid discrimination in the community at large (Miami, Dade County)?

A response to this assignment by Kenric Leach follows this essay. I was pleased with the outcome of this lesson. My students were enthusiastic researchers. Their previous responses to discrimination had been merely emotional. They now were interested in discovering how discrimination was addressed legally in our democratic society.

This lesson began with the examination of personal feelings about prejudice and racism, moved on to the study of prejudice and racism in literature, then to the investigation through research of the legality of discrimination. At each step in the lesson students were given the opportunity to discuss and respond in writing to the topic. This three-week lesson was an excellent introduction to our nine-week Connections project.

The Pen Pal Exchange

The students were introduced to the Connections project during the second nine-week period of the school year in order to give me time at the beginning of the year to establish a rapport with the students and to create a classroom climate of comfort and trust. The students had a predictably negative initial reaction to the pen pal exchange, which neither surprised nor worried me. They argued that they felt uncomfortable writing personal letters to strangers. One student ("D") remarked in a journal entry:

November 22
Today I wrote my first pen pal letter to my pen pal. I don't really want to have a pen pal but we have to for class. Maybe after the ice is broken I might like her. For now, I disagree with the idea.

Another student ("A") journal reveals the disappointment in her assigned pen pal:

Journal Entry #4
We all received our pen pal names today. I wound up with a white boy. Well I didn't get what I wanted. He has a dorky name . . . Sounds like a bookworm, Jew, who is short and skinny! Doesn't sound like a dreamboat to me. I hope he really isn't like that!

These entries show the students' lack of enthusiasm and flexibility. I knew they needed time to "establish ties," as the fox reminds the Little Prince in the novel *The Little Prince*. The students' attitudes did, in fact, change over time. After having received a letter, notice the change in "D's" attitude:

December 12
Today I received my first pen pal letter. I think I might like her after all. If she wrote back to me after what I wrote in the letter I sent, I know she must be a nice person. At first I felt weird writing to someone I do not know—but now I think it is for the best!

And "A" was pleasantly surprised as well:

Journal Entry #5
We got our letters back today. Not everyone got theirs. Well, [the pen pal] seems to be an alright person. He's going to FSU in the fall. I like FSU. He also plays the piano. I play the piano. He also plays tennis. His mom just redid their house and so did mine! He likes heavy metal. Yuck!!! I like Rap and R&B music. He's not perfect but he's O.K. We'll see how the second letter goes! I can't wait.

The hands-on, experiential summer training reminded me that preaching that those "others" are human beings, too, is not as effective as allowing students to experience "inhabiting other lives" themselves.

Throughout the weeks students corresponded with their pen pals; they sent a literary greeting card (a card designed or written in the persona of a character from a work studied in class) and an artistic mandala (a symbolic representation of their perception of their pen pal's personality). Each Friday we shared feelings about values in a "boundary breaking" human relations circle. And as students studied works by authors such as Antoine de Saint Exupéry, Elie Wiesel, Maya Angelou, James Baldwin, and Gabriel García Márquez while corresponding with their pen pals, something quite miraculous happened in the classroom. Students no longer tolerated racial slurs made by classmates. They would consciously stop one another. The classroom became a self-healing kind of environment. After having truly "inhabited other lives," we were not the same people who had begun the project. As the fox taught the Little Prince, we learned together "What is essential is invisible to the eye."

The personal changes our students made through experience and increased awareness are best summed up by Kenric Leach, who noted in a journal entry:

> November 29
>
> Today I went to a nursing home on Biscayne Boulevard. My interaction with the senior citizens is not the topic of this entry, but my interaction with those of the opposite race.
>
> Background: About 20 of us set out for the nursing home in 3 cars. On the way there, however, one of the cars overheated. Therefore, one of the two remaining cars had to shuttle the rest of the people in the third car to the nursing home.
>
> When it came time to leave, four of us had to be left behind because there were only two cars. It was me, Paul, Tommy and Louis. While we were waiting, we talked about and brought up stereotypes about blacks and whites (Tommy and Paul are white, I'm black, and Louis is of mixed race). The four of us, or at least I, realized that he could take no side in the race discussion, and no stereotype could stick to him. Afterwards, we began to play basketball and goof around. At that point, we lost our color, our class ranking, our height, our backgrounds. We were just four kids goofing around. I think that this is the way it should always be.

The Legacy of Discrimination: Who Pays the Cost?
Kenric Leach

In most people's minds, discrimination is almost automatically seen on a sexual or racial plane. When thinking of discrimination, we think of a black man being denied access to a restaurant or store because of his race, or a woman being denied a job even though her credentials are superior to the man who was hired. Though racial and sexual discrimination are the most prevalent in our society, they are not the only kinds. Each case of discrimination, in a sense, must be seen on a personal aspect. To me, discrimination is never being picked for football, or basketball, or any sport, because of my height—or lack of height. To a handicapped person, discrimination may be the lack of ramps or elevators in public places. To an elderly person, it may be being denied a proper education because he was born in the poorhouse instead of the penthouse. Whatever the discrimination may be, the reason is always ignorance and always a result of the prejudice which runs rampant in our society and our world.

Though cases of racial and/or sexual discrimination are sometimes in the news, no full-time attention is given to these problems or the many other types of discrimination in our society. It always takes some kind of murder or robbery with racist overtones for discrimination to come into the national focus. Unfortunately, it takes only a matter of weeks, the situation is forgotten and life returns to normal. The same is true in case of sexual harassment. Once the cases are tried, the decisions, which are few and far between, are forgotten and lost in the law books. As for discriminatory problems concerning age, physical condition, or social status, there is no voice crying out against these atrocities. If there is a voice for these people, it is certainly very faint. There is definitely room for improvement in addressing these issues.

It seems that many people do not understand the concept of improvement in terms of discrimination. Improvement means more active speakers continually addressing that many persons are denied employment, housing, and access to public places on account of sex, color, race, religion, physical condition, or social status. Improvement means the installation of ramps and/or elevators for the physically handicapped. Improvement means affirmative action for those with "hidden handicaps," such as diabetes, epilepsy, heart disease, etc. Improvement means the enforcement of the anti-discrimination laws which, at present, stand idle in the United States Code. As is very often true, the resources—or in this case, the legislation—are there, but are not being used. It is time for our legislators to silence their hollow and meaningless words, and prove that actions speak louder —and clearer—than words.

Though they are not enforced very often, there are numerous laws against discrimination in the United States. The most influential of the statutes are contained in the United States Code. The Civil Rights Act of 1964, which is documented in Title 42, subtitle 2000e of the Code, prohibits discrimination on account of race, color, religion, or national origin. Sexual discrimination is prohibited by Section 6d of the Fair Labor Standards Act of 1938 (Title 29, subtitle 206d). Discrimination in employment on the basis of handicap, physical or "hidden," is prohibited by Section 501 of the Rehabili-tation Act of 1973 (Title 29, subtitle 791). Discrimination in employment on account of age is prohibited by the Age Discrimination in Employment Act of 1967 (Title 29, sub-title 631, 633a). Though these laws prohibit discrimination of any kind, they are seldom enforced. Either this is because American society has become less prejudicial in practice (which is doubtful) or because no one is bringing cases of discrimination into the court-room. A conscious observer would lean toward the latter of the two.

Who suffers most from the practice of discrimination? In my opinion, both parties, the victim and the perpetrator, are equally damaged. Obviously, the victim suffers because discrimination undermines self-esteem and confidence. Although some people may be less sensitive to discrimination than others, they are affected subconsciously. Sooner or later, the less sensitive victim will eventually become as frustrated as the victim who reacts immediately. On the same note, the perpetrator suffers because he or she lives in a world of ignorance, and will never take the time to learn the truth because of this. So, as one can see, discrimination and its aftereffects are equally destructive and detrimental to the perpetrator and the victim. Therefore, the only true and effective method for stop-ping the ripples of discrimination and prejudice is never to start them.

In my opinion, in order to change the community at large, it is necessary to tackle it in my own sphere of influence. I must try to eliminate any prejudices I may have against anyone I know and/or with whom I am acquainted. I truly believe that if everyone does the same thing, the spheres of influence will overlap and slowly change in the communi-ty will be seen. It may take years to achieve a prejudice-free society in this way, and it may never happen in my lifetime. However, we can hope that a difference can be made by simply learning more about someone and sharing a little of yourself in the process. I believe that it can, and will, be done.

Comments on "Inhabiting Other Lives"
Dixie Goswami

Carol Green recalls the development of a new unit for her tenth-grade honors English students at Miami Norland Senior High School. Drawing from her own intellectual and emotional experiences as a participant in a summer humanities institute, she designed a unit that invited students to read, talk, and write about humanities texts that promote new understandings of diversity and reduce ethnic and racial prejudice. Green shows how she created a context for responding to "Crackling Day" by Peter Abrahams and "After You, My Dear Alphonse" by Shirley Jackson that included:

- Close reading of the texts.
- Firsthand experiences in the community.
- Library research.
- Journal writing, essay, fiction, and poetry writing.
- Letter writing exchanges between students with different ethnic and cultural backgrounds.
- Much discussion and conversation.

Green's account illustrates the key elements that contributed to her planning; chief among them were her summer study of multicultural humanities texts and her commitment to opening the curriculum to texts and activities that acknowledge ethnic diversity, with the explicit goal of reducing prejudice and racism.

Student Writing as Multicultural Texts

It would be easy to categorize Kenric Leach's essay, poem, and journal writing as an example of what honors students can do routinely that is far removed from the thinking, reading, writing, and understanding of ordinary young people. But most students, including unsuccessful, reluctant students, are capable in certain environments of being thoughtful readers and powerful writers. Green's reading of her students' texts—her treating their essays, poems, and journal entries as multicultural humanities texts—affects the content of her students' writings and the ways they use written language. One of our most important tasks as teachers is to represent to students the quality of their thought, to read and respond to their writing and art so as to give our interpretations back to the child or young person—these interactions promote fresh learning and language development.

Dixie Goswami is a professor of English at Clemson University and coordinator of the Program in Writing, Bread Loaf School of English, Middlebury College. She is director of a national project called "Writing for the Community" funded by the Bingham Trust. She is coeditor of *Reclaiming the Classroom: Teacher Research as an Agency for Change* (1985) and *Students Teaching/Teachers Learning* (1992).

I'd like to read a fully detailed account of Kenric's composition of "The Legacy," to see how the writing evolved from concept to final draft and how the process was embedded in classroom talk, writing, and reading. While it is clear that Green expects students to produce a wide range of writings, some carefully researched and edited, she reads Kenric Leach for meaning and understanding, in order to "inhabit other lives," just as she reads Jackson, Abrahams, and other writers.

I'm suggesting that the inclusion of students' writings—especially when students have different backgrounds, languages, and histories—as classroom texts that offer up images, stories, and information about diversity must be a key feature of successful multicultural humanities education. I want to emphasize that this rich, interactive climate for learning, including challenging and complex texts, is appropriate for all tenth-graders. All young people.

The fashioning of a new classroom culture is not easy. Teachers and young people must struggle to retain and appreciate cultural diversity and at the same time read common texts and develop a common language for writing, speaking, and succeeding academically. Green calls on her students' language and culture as valued resources for reading, writing, and critical thinking about texts and about prejudice and racism. In the pen-pal exchange and in other activities, Green uses the language and culture of the students in her teaching, thereby expanding and enriching the way her students

- read and respond to literature;
- study historical events such as the Civil Rights Act of 1964;
- describe and reflect on their own experience—as Kenric Leach remembers his visit to a Biscayne Boulevard nursing home and the pen pals reflect on the weirdness of writing to a stranger;
- and acknowledge the meaningfulness of their lived experience.

Organizations such as CHART and teachers such as Carol Green help us explore in practical terms how students' linguistic and cultural differences function as important and necessary starting points for high-quality, democratic education.

Transforming Narratives

Narratives such as Green's are significant as documents that help us understand how and why change occurs (from the teacher's perspective) and what change means to teachers and students. One way to promote the study of multicultural humanities texts is to provide study guides and curriculum materials. Another, the Connections way, is to provide teachers with quality opportunities for professional renewal and for classroom research to

1. study texts with colleagues, scholars, and others;
2. apply what Green calls their intellectual and emotional experiences to their particular situations;
3. document, reflect on, and interpret what actually happens by looking closely at a single student or at key features of the lesson or program;
4. write about their impressions and analyses.

Moreover, Green's account provides us with a context for assessment, especially portfolio assessment. Ideally, we would collect narratives from all participants in the Inhabiting Other Lives summer institute to study and learn from—and we would acknowledge the importance of these teacher texts. Without these accounts, even with national standards and tests, we lose the opportunity to think critically about theory, practice, and the assumptions that underlie efforts to improve schooling for all children. An important measure of the Miami project's success is that Green is extremely articulate about what she has done and why, how she has done it, and what doing it has "meant" within the Miami Norland context.

Praxis: Action, Reflection, and Change

Carol and the members of her Connections team asked serious questions about what was being taught in their classrooms, how it was taught, and what should constitute the larger goals of education. Their concerns about racism and prejudice were informed by the academic perspectives of disciplines such as history and literature: they—and their students—were politicized.

It's easy to imagine Kenric Leach raising some tough questions as a result of his studying and writing about discrimination in Dade County and elsewhere. He might want to know more about why victims of discrimination aren't routinely bringing large numbers of cases into the courtroom. Or if and why the laws have been weakened or struck down and by what process. Since Kenric Leach believes that individual responsibility is the key to eliminating prejudice, he may insist on trying to identify local discriminatory structures and practices. The odds are good that he'll want to read narratives and historical studies related to the legacy of discrimination. He may want to read poetry that's thematically related to his poem, "Red, White, and Blue." Speaking more generally, will Kenric and his fellow students resist a "neutral" humanities curriculum, if they should be presented with one? Will their inquiries and intentions be honored and supported by their teachers, their schools, or their communities?

CHART projects articulate critical questions for researchers and at the same time provide settings for studies that need to be conducted: CHART has the potential for involving teachers in all aspects of research, which is as critical a component of professional development as content- and pedagogy-specific workshops and institutes.

I'd like to ask Kenric and other students whose teachers were in the Connections project to talk about their perceptions of the extent to which programs like Green's promote tolerance and nonracist behavior. Might these students wish to be called upon to help design units and to serve as pen pals, discussion leaders, and evaluators? We know about the power of clubs, writing and reading groups, and similar organizations to engage students over long periods of time in serious and productive work. Quality content and critical classroom practice aren't the only issues: giving students real options to work meaningfully and informally in small groups, with an adult—over time—is a top priority, if social constructionist theories of language and learning are to be applied and tested. Again, Green's project demonstrates that CHART presents opportunities to study critical issues about the consequences of multicultural humanities teaching and learning.

Multicultural Humanities Education as Process

Multicultural humanities education is a process. I'm eager to ask Green to speculate about the next stage. Given her experiences in the classroom after the Connections project, the diversity of her own school and classroom, and the many constraints that she must deal with, I wonder if she and her new students will try to develop a list (and a classroom library) of humanities texts from Jamaican, Bahamian, Caribbean, and other writers to read and respond to. What will the pen-pal exchange look like next year? How will the students' texts be read, collected, published, and "used"? Will students who aren't in honors classes be able to participate? Is Green in touch with Dale Gary, Jose Piedra, Haywood Randolph, and Joel Schackne? With scholars and members of the project staff? Will she be encouraged, if she's so inclined, to form and lead a Miami Norland Inhabit Other Lives project?

After CHART

Over the past few decades, many fine programs have been created to bring scholars and teachers together. Most have been funded by private foundations or special grants. There's little evidence that colleges and universities and school districts have seen these disciplinary-based working alliances as central to their mission, appearing in annual budgets rather than depending on grants. It is surely easier to continue traditional in-service and professional education programs, especially the packaged kind, than to do the restructuring and reconceptualizing that would assure Green and members of her team the opportunities to work with scholars and one another on projects that promote curricular change and critical pedagogy. Perhaps the nonhierarchical, built-in diversity of the projects (in part the basis of their success) militates against them when it comes to finding institutionalized support.

Teachers, scholars, and project leaders should not continue to have too depend for the most part on outside funding for sustaining programs that contribute to achieving local, state, and national goals. Budgets are tight: it's never a good time to ask questions about money, but it's necessary to determine the chances of projects such as this one for becoming priority items—now or later. I am encouraged when I read about local, state, or national plans for school change, many of which include elaborate plans for including teachers in making decisions about curriculum, school management, and so on, but where are the states and districts and the colleges and universities that take seriously teacher scholarship and research as a key tool for school reform? Where are the states and districts and colleges and universities that build on privately funded programs such as CHART and institutionalize support over a long period of time to establish research and scholarly communities? Perhaps that kind of support is a possibility in Miami.

Carol Green's story about Inhabiting Other Lives has obviously just begun.

History is not what it used to be: the relentless march of the names and dates that chronicled the advance of European culture and institutions into the "New World" that became America. In its place in schools is a growing acknowledgement that this particular "history" is only one of a vast number of tales that deserve telling; that the processes of conducting a historical inquiry are perhaps more important for a student to grasp than any particular set of dates or "facts"; and that just as today's classrooms are composed of children from a wide range of ethnic, cultural and racial backgrounds, so too is the real story of American (and world) history.

A number of CHART projects focus specifically on history, and most include some engagement with historical information. We have selected several essays that reflect some of the core ideas CHART holds about history as a living discipline, full of rich and exciting information about human culture. The **PATHS World History Project**, developed by the Philadelphia Alliance for Teaching Humanities in the Schools (PATHS), has created a new curriculum in World History rooted in chronology and geography, exploring comparative change in diverse civilizations. This curriculum is the result of an on-going process linking teachers and scholars. The **Rural Education Alliance for Collaborative Humanities (REACH)** in South Carolina approaches history in a very broad and inclusive way: nurturing teacher-led projects that link the discovery of local history and culture with writing activities, oral history collection, and community celebration. The **Connecticut Humanities Alliance** encourages educational change through the development of interdisciplinary curricula created collaboratively by teachers, scholars, historical societies and cultural institutions. The **Superintendent's Academy for Humanities and Arts Teaching** in Washington, D.C. uses important aspects of African American history—among a wide range of other topics—to help students discover their own identities, and to make school an affirming place to be.

A key feature of each of these projects is an attempt to help children see some aspects of themselves in history. Each project uses its own methods to cultivate this personal connection to historical material—having students write imaginative first-person narratives putting themselves in a historical context they have studied, focusing on local or family histories, or making an effort to include some of the histories of the racial, ethnic or cultural groups represented by the students in the classroom. Embedded in each of these efforts is an explicit belief that students will become more interested in learning about history, if it can be brought to life for them.

Illustration by Keith Schmiedlin.

Pharaoh's Dreams . . . and Ours
James Culbertson

In some high-school history classes, students are rarely, if ever, asked to synthesize the material they are memorizing. They are usually asked to make sense of historical events only in terms of their chronological order, or as manifestations of shifts of political and economic power. They often view the subject of their history classes as a succession of meaningless names and dates. They see the role of the historian as little more than that of a chronicler. Their lack of engagement with the subject results in a kind of "So what!" attitude that leaves them historically illiterate after the three years of mandatory high-school courses. Not only indifference, but outright resentment was expressed by students who listed history as their least favorite subject in a recent poll.

The World History Project in Philadelphia is made up primarily of teachers who have been teaching in the Philadelphia system for fifteen years or more. The majority of us have not been trained as historians. We hold degrees in social studies education, sociology, and political science rather than in history. Yet we are acutely aware of the lack of responsiveness to history exhibited by most of our students. Some of us dreamed of enlivening our classrooms by engaging students in seeing themselves as historians making sense of the past. We dreamed of changing our students' view of history by changing the way we taught it. Those of us who shared this dream banded together under the auspices of PATHS/PRISM—The Philadelphia Partnership for Education—to reinvent Philadelphia's World History curriculum.

PATHS/PRISM

PATHS/PRISM—acronyms for the Philadelphia Alliance for Teaching Humanities in the Schools, and the Philadelphia Renaissance in Science and Mathematics—is a CHART-affiliated organization. It is one of the nation's largest, most comprehensive public-private partnerships in support of public education. PATHS/PRISM was founded in 1984 at the request of Superintendent Constance E. Clayton and has played an increasingly central role in her mission of excellence for the School District of Philadelphia. PATHS/PRISM has successfully brought together the resources of the local corporate, university, scientific, and cultural communities to provide Philadelphia educators K-12 with top-quality, innovative staff and curriculum development programs designed to improve arts, humanities, science, and math instruction in the city's schools. Fifth-largest in the nation,

James Culbertson is the Social Studies department head at Benjamin Franklin High School in Philadelphia. He holds a B.A. in History and Humanities from San Francisco State University and an M.Ed. from Temple University. He served as the Curriculum Design Team Leader for the PATHS World History Project. Mr. Culbertson's teaching has been recognized with the ARCO Chemical Award for dedication to teaching (1989) and the Mordechai Anielewisc Award for dedication to teaching the lessons of the Holocaust (1988).

the School District of Philadelphia serves almost 200,000 students—78 percent of whom are members of a minority group—and employs more than 10,000 classroom teachers.

In addition to the World History Project, PATHS/PRISM's programs in the humanities have included a highly acclaimed districtwide Writing across the Curriculum program, with funding for each school to carry out a writing project; an American History project that introduced teachers to selected topics in local and national history; and a summer institute that introduced middle-school teachers to the use of literature and film in teaching about cultural diversity.

The World History Project

In January 1988, PATHS/PRISM brought together eighty teachers, administrators, and curriculum specialists from the School District of Philadelphia to begin a study of the way the ancient world was being taught. During this meeting the World History Project was born. We formed committees, plotted directions for further investigation, and went to work meeting regularly in large group sessions to report on our progress. We worked with university professors from the immediate area, as well as with national authorities. Together, we began to carve out a new way of looking at and teaching an old body of knowledge.

We understood that we had to take on the role of students as we studied not only various ancient civilizations, but also the linkages among them. We realized that our own knowledge of history was limited to the Eurocentric history courses that had been *de rigueur* during our college years. If we were to open up our World History classes to include non-Western civilizations, the lives of ordinary people, or the role of women, then we would have to rethink history ourselves.

As our view of World History became more sophisticated, we realized that the prevailing concept of curricular "scope and sequence" was inadequate. The ninth-grade World History course outlined in the school district's *Instructional Planning Guide* focused almost entirely on the political, economic, and military history of Western Europe. Since this course of study mimicked the organization of the most commonly used world history textbooks, instruction was driven by the need to cover the chapters and units in these books, and student learning was defined in terms of memorizing and recalling information.

What emerged to replace this old course of study was a world history curriculum with a "warp and woof" that mirrored the multidimensional fabric of history. The new course of study was organized both chronologically and thematically around eight topics: early humans, cities, empires, belief systems, trade, human migration, revolution, and technology. Through this course of study, we sought to create a global world history that included people from all strata of society.

We also came to realize that what we wanted students to be able to do was to investigate the role of continuity and change over time. Instead of concentrating on imparting information to students, our new curriculum centered on getting students to formulate questions about the past and to seek answers to them. In the process of planning how to do this, we discovered that less could be more.

It was clear that if more material was to be added to the already overwhelming prehistory-to-the-present span of World History, more time would be necessary in the high-school schedule. The project teachers agreed that the World History curriculum would have to be expanded from a one-year to a two-year course, with the first year spent studying the Ancient World (human origins through the rise of trade, around 1400 A.D.), and the second year spent studying the Modern World (the beginning of the rise of trade through the present).

Ultimately, the dream at the heart of the World History Project was translated into expectations for student learning and achievement.

• Students must study history in a whole-world context.

• Students should be aware of multiple perspectives and be able to use a variety of primary resources in studying history.

• Students must engage actively in the work of historians, continually asking the questions "What do we know?" and "How do we know it?"

• Students must discover the relevance of the study of history to their own lives.

Superintendent Clayton was enthusiastic about a teacher-directed revamping of the World History requirements. In fact, Dr. Clayton's embrace of the World History Project and her enthusiasm for its innovative approaches have been an important impetus in piloting the project, as it grew to include more than thirty-five secondary schools. She confirmed that the Ancient World course of the World History Project would be the mandated history course for freshmen in Philadelphia. The Modern World has become an elective history course.

Benjamin Franklin High School

During the 1990–91 school year, I taught the Ancient World component of the World History Project curriculum to a ninth-grade class at Benjamin Franklin High School. Franklin is an inner-city comprehensive high school located in North Philadelphia. It is the high school of last resort for students in that neighborhood: that is to say, it is attended only by those students not recruited to attend one of the magnet high schools or whose parents have not sought an alternative setting for them. Only about 63 percent of the one thousand or so students are in attendance on any given day. Sixty percent of the students live near or below the poverty level, and a similar percentage function below the national norms in reading and mathematics. The dropout rate is thought to be one of the highest in the city. If the new program could work to engage these students in history, then it could probably work with students anywhere else in the city.

The Rise of Cities

The second unit of the World History curriculum has as its theme an investigation of the rise of cities. It focuses on the period from 3500–1000 B.C. and on the geographic regions of the Nile and Indus River Valleys, China, West Africa, Mesopotamia, Meso-America, Southeast Asia, and the eastern Mediterranean basin. As part of our inquiry into the rise of cities, I asked my ninth-grade World History students to read a section of

Ross Dunn's *World History—Links across Time and Place* textbook in which he ties the development of cities to the rise of civilizations.[1] As we discussed Dunn's concept of "civilization," we compared it to what we knew about cities from living in Philadelphia. When I encouraged students to challenge assertions in the textbook by comparing them to their own experience, they developed a hypothesis that mirrored the one in the textbook.

> Conditions for a Civilization
> Full-time specialization of labor
> A structure of social classes
> Settlement in cities that serve as shrines, citadels, and markets
> A system of government
> A system of writing
> A shared "worldview"

The students seemed incapable of envisioning any new criteria.

Pharaoh's Dreams

To test—and to expand—their hypothesis of a civilization, I decided to use a piece of classical literature: the passage from the book of Genesis in the Bible in which Joseph interprets Pharaoh's dreams.[2] I made it clear that we were reading the biblical text as a primary source, and not as a religious document. We would not debate the religious aspects of the text. Instead, we would be combing the narrative for details of an ancient society.

As we began to read the passage aloud and to discuss it together, I was struck by the number of students who did not know the story of Joseph. Only two or three students in the class could associate Joseph with the multicolored coat his father, Jacob, had given him. Only one knew the story of how Joseph got to Egypt. No one knew how Joseph had ended up in an Egyptian jail. I briefly outlined the story of Joseph. Not surprisingly, the episode involving Potiphar's wife's attempt to seduce Joseph motivated at least a half a dozen students to read more of the Bible on their own.

When we had finished reading and discussing the selection, I asked the students to list the occupations that were mentioned in the story. They were to note how many times and for what reasons Joseph changed his clothes. They had to list the symbols of power that were given to Joseph by Pharaoh, and to describe the significance of each of the symbols. Finally, using the criteria they had generated, the students had to determine whether Egypt was a civilization. In other words, I was asking them to give me evidence that their theory about civilizations was a valid one. This is the kind of thinking that high-school students are not usually asked to do in their history classes.

This kind of a classroom activity was new both to the students and to me. I had used literature in my classroom before, to supplement the textbook, a sort of "see-what-I-mean" approach. Now students were using a literary text to test their own hypothesis, one which they had developed through reading other primary sources and through observation of their own society. I was surprised at the depth of the students' responses.

The Joseph text was a rich resource for students. Arguing from the text, they thought that occupations such as assistant cup-bearer (Joseph's cellmate in prison who eventually brings him to Pharaoh as a dream interpreter) suggested a specialization of labor and a social hierarchy. Students argued that Joseph's wardrobe changes—from his bath and shave before being presented to Pharaoh, to his new clothes after being named viceroy—indicated the importance of clothing as an indicator of social class. They believed that the symbols of Joseph's power (the ring, chain, wife, chariot, and Egyptian name) demonstrated the existence of a governmental system and a common worldview in Egypt.

As a result of reading the Joseph story, the students were becoming more articulate. They became absorbed in the process of thinking about the concept of civilization. They expressed a need to modify their definition of a civilization. They speculated that a civilization such as Egypt must have had agricultural surpluses, and argued that if this were not the case, then everyone would have been engaged in subsistence farming. Since in the Joseph story there is evidence of both the existence of surpluses and of a ruling class that controls them, students felt that surpluses were necessary to support diversified and specialized labor and complex governmental systems. They also thought that surpluses were necessary for the development of long-distance trade. Students cited Joseph's brothers traveling to Egypt to buy grain as support for this conclusion.

The students decided that a knowledge of arithmetic, geometry, and astronomy was also a necessary element of a civilization. Their evidence for this was the ability of the Egyptians to calculate the seven fruitful years during which they should be storing grain. They argued that knowledge of astronomy and mathematics is a prerequisite for developing a calendar. The students already knew that the Egyptians had built temples and pyramids, and they suggested that these edifices were further evidence of the use of arithmetic and, especially, geometry.

Since there were obviously places to store the surplus grain from the seven fruitful years, students held that any civilization that had agricultural surpluses might also have monumental public buildings. Again, the students already knew that the Egyptians had built temples and pyramids. Students proposed that these edifices were evidence that monumental public buildings are a distinguishing feature of civilizations.

What I was seeing was not only increased participation and involvement, but also the emergence of the students' voices in my classroom. They were engaged in discussion and debate, and it was on the topic we were studying! They were acting like true historians—examining a written text and asking questions: What sense can we make of this? What can we assume? What is the validity of any assumption we make? How do we check? They were able to ask the questions as well as to give the answers. I was surprised and delighted, and so were they. This was what I had dreamed of having happen in my classroom.

Students as Explorers

As a result of their reading, writing, and discussion, a new consensus emerged concerning the necessary conditions for a civilization. They formulated a new list:

Conditions for a Civilization (Revised)
Settlement in cities that serve as shrines, citadels, and markets
Full-time specialization of labor
Concentration of surpluses
A structure of social classes
A system of government
Monumental public works
Long-distance trade
A system of writing
A shared "worldview"
Knowledge of arithmetic, geometry, and astronomy

Next, I asked the students to pretend that they were explorers who traveled to a new place and encountered a group of people. They were to write three journal entries corresponding to three days of exploration. Their descriptions should *show* that this group of people had a complex civilization, according to their new criteria. Using their lists, the class went to work. The list provided just enough of a scaffold for them to build the more detailed description of an imaginary story. As noisy as the discussions had been, this was the quietest time I had experienced with this class.

After the students had finished writing, I organized the class into small groups. I asked the students in each group to read their journal entries and to critique them. After each paper was read, students made suggestions about what to add and what to leave out. They questioned one another about meaning and discussed how to best express that meaning. After the small groups had finished, I asked students to revise their papers. Finally, I invited students to read their finished papers to the whole class.

Margarita Olivio was one of the first to volunteer. Margarita, a fourteen-year-old freshman, was an average student who generally did not volunteer readily. She good-naturedly tolerated her classmates' kidding, but as the only Latina in a class composed of African Americans, she made it clear that she was not prepared to take abuse from anyone—especially from the girls. Her responses to the assignment were typical of the papers I received.

The First Day

Dear Journal,

We were shipwrecked in the storm on some tropical island of which I overheard the crew and the captain saying that this island is not located on his map. I am the only woman that was on board the ship. I am their slave girl. The captain noticed another woman hiding, spying from the bushes. They captured her and was holding her captive until a large group of women came to her capture. A fight broke out and more women came. Soon all of the men were over powered by the women. I was hiding in the bushes for fear of being killed. I noticed that all of the women were dressed the same. When all of the men were chained in shackles, six men also chained in shackles came to the group of women warriors baring on their shoulders a sedan chair. They placed the sedan chair on the ground. A woman appeared from under the canopy covering. At the sight of her all of the other women kneeled on the ground and bowed their heads to her. She spoke to them. She was speaking very good English for an islander. I sneezed from under the bushes. The woman heard the noise and noticed the movement in the bushes. A group of women headed my way and I fainted.

Margarita Olivo

The Second Day

Dear Journal,

I awoke the next day on a cushioned cot-like bed. Two men hovered over me with a large branch from a tree covered with leaves fanning me. I almost screamed when I came to my full senses. The woman that the other women were worshiping came to me. I was at a loss for words. I didn't know what I was supposed to do and I think she knew it. She spoke to me. She said, "My name ia Maliaka. I am the queen of this island. This island that you have settled on is called Killawa." The woman had a strong accent that I couldn't recognize. We spoke for a long period of time. She told me all about the island and I told her about my life as a slave. She said that the men were to be punished. A man came to her with a large book with weird squiggles drawn in it. She grabbed the container with black liquid inside and with the point of a stem from a leaf she drew more squiggles. I asked what she was doing and she said that she was writing the men's punishment down. She gave the book to the man and another came with a large tray of food, so we ate and went to bed.

Margarita Olivo

The Third Day

Dear Journal,

Today, I awoke and I was escorted by a young boy to a large pool of water. Other women were bathing within the water, so I joined them. After bathing, Queen Maliaka gave me some clothing much like her's. She gave me a tour of the island. She showed me where they keep their extra food stored. She introduced me to the other women who were in charge of the men who did the hard labor. She showed me a parchment that had those funny squiggles on them. She told me that the parchment read how many times the sun and moon showed and when the sun would come and when the moon would come. Next, she took me to a place where many of the women were gathered and showed me a statue made of pure gold of me. She introduced me to all of the women as the next queen of the island and they all bowed to me. At that moment, I knew my life here would be wonderful.

Margarita Olivo

Margarita's journal entries were insightful and thought-provoking. She was able to synthesize most, if not all, of the criteria for a civilization into a very readable presentation that was somehow evocative of the biblical passage we had read. Her emphasis on gender roles led us into a heated discussion about the inclusion of gender roles in our criteria for defining a civilization. On one hand, the boys suspected that gender roles are either unimportant or that they are somehow genetically determined. On the other hand, the girls were passionately convinced that gender roles are culturally determined and that they change as civilizations become more complex. The debate was lively, though the class was not disappointed that the question was never resolved. I feel strongly that Margarita's journal entries and the classes' involvement with this topic would never have happened in a classroom where students' observations and assumptions were not valued and explored.

Pharaoh and I both have dreams of prosperous years. He dreamed of fat cows and fields full of grain. I dream of classes full of eager students. For him, the years of plenty preceded the lean years. For me, it was the other way around.

Notes

1. Ross E. Dunn. *World History—Links across Time and Place* (Evanston, Il.: McDougell, Littell and Company, 1988), pp. 26–29.

2. Genesis 41:1–57. *Tanakh: A New Translation of the Holy Scriptures According to the Traditional Hebrew Text* (Philadelphia, PA: The Jewish Publication Society, 1985), pp. 64–67.

Comments on "Pharaoh's Dreams . . . and Ours"
Stanley N. Katz

I think it would be wonderful to be a student in James Culbertson's World History classes on the ancient world. We have, of course, been teaching something called World History for many years, but it has tended to be a lengthy and uncomplicated chronological approach to Near Eastern and European history, culminating in the settlement of the "New World," with side glances at Far Eastern civilizations. For the most part, then, World History really was what might more properly have been called Western Civilization, and although this is was a useful exercise for any American student, it cannot suffice in today's interconnected world.

Culbertson and his colleagues at PATHS/PRISM have clearly tapped into the "new" World History, which aims to start even before recorded history (that is, verbal records), to cover at least a sample of all of the world's "civilizations," and to explore the contrasts and connections among different patterns of living. This movement is also taking root, though more weakly, in higher education, but aside from a few very good textbooks, such as Ross Dunn's *World History—Links Across Time and Place*, used in the Culbertson class, teachers must create their own classroom materials and lessons. This is a problem, but, as Culbertson shows, it is also a tremendous pedagogical opportunity.

The challenge is to sensitize today's high-school students to the vast varieties of human experience that might be labeled "civilized" and to help them locate their cultures in relationship to larger geographical and temporal patterns. This process of self-conscious historical self-location is obviously of increasing importance as the United States becomes ever more multicultural, for in many of our schools only a minority of students trace their roots to Europe. This is clearly the case in Culbertson's school.

Culbertson's essay describing his experience in teaching a unit in the World History course on the rise of cities gives some indication of the intellectual breadth of the course the PATHS/PRISM teachers are developing—it ranges from the Near East to Africa, Middle America, Southeast Asia, and the Mediterranean, and covers two and a half millennia. One has to guess that the teachers forgo chronological and other kinds of "facts" in favor of a much more general and principled approach to understanding historic civilizations and their relations to one another. This technique, of course, always creates conflict in history reform, for there will always be those who insist that facts are the sole basis of history; they argue that the only thing that counts is "how much seventeen-year-olds know," defining knowledge in a crudely empirical manner. This is nonsense, since the very notion of "fact" has been called into question for good intellectual reasons, and the reality is that students can learn and retain only so much empirical data, and they generally find the rote learning required quite boring. It is much more important that students have an understanding of the "essence" of history—how things change over

Historian Stanley N. Katz is President of the American Council of Learned Societies, and is a Senior Fellow of the Woodrow Wilson School of Public and International Affairs, Princeton University.

time—in order to have a way to reason historically. Teaching history conceptually is not only more durable and useful, it is also more fun for both teacher and student.

The exercise Culbertson describes in the essay does not seem to have much to do with how things change over time, but it is only one lesson in his approach to World History. What the lesson does is to demonstrate how a secondary school teacher can begin to convey to at-risk students something of the substance of history, some feeling for the fabric of human experience. Culbertson is working with a set of general principles (proposed by Dunn in his textbook) about the preconditions for civilization. He has asked his students to derive conclusions from a surprisingly unfamiliar biblical text, using it as the actual record ("fact") of a historical experience. This must have been jarring to students more accustomed to thinking of the Bible as a revealed religious text, and probably almost entirely unprepared to think of it as a historical document. What does the Bible tell, Culbertson asks his students, about Egypt at a particular point in time? From his description, it sounds as though they began to understand what it means to derive both fact and interpretation from a particular historical text, and this, to my way of thinking, is much more important than learning packaged details about "Egyptian Civilization." They are beginning to think historically.

The students used the data they derived from the biblical text to critique Dunn's criteria for civilizations, adding some new criteria of their own, surely a useful and creative intellectual exercise. But I confess that I am troubled about this aspect of Culbertson's approach. The rigid nature of Dunn's criteria for the establishment of civilizations strikes me as extremely artificial, rather a throwback to Arnold Toynbee's notions of civilization, and all too general for most historical purposes. Indeed, I do not believe that the very concept of "civilization" is intellectually appropriate, since it implies a hierarchy of cultures that does not obviously belong in a "new" World History course. Nevertheless, it does seem apparent that the students were engaged by the discussion, and that they doubtless were thereby impelled to think more seriously about the nature of earlier patterns of human life. Whatever my intellectual misgivings, however, these students were thinking about history in a critical way.

The writing exercises must have been extraordinarily successful, for Margarita Olivio's essay is extraordinary. It reveals quite a lot about her own thoughts about identity, particularly as a woman, but it also shows that she has developed a very nice appreciation for the general lesson about civilization that Culbertson was trying to convey. Quite frankly, her essay strikes me as more useful for its emotional and developmental contribution to the student's life than as an essay about history, and I myself would prefer to see something rooted a little more closely to the actual nature of historic experience. Nevertheless, it seems to me altogether likely that Margarita Olivio will have been impelled to think seriously about ancient civilizations and to approach the rest of the course with enhanced enthusiasm.

The Culbertson materials are a dramatic indication of how an intelligent teacher, well equipped to consider new approaches to an old subject, can produce materials and strategies to draw his students into historical thinking in a highly effective way. As I have indicated, I would have emphasized different themes and stressed different intellectual strategies, but I have no difficulty in recognizing in Culbertson a truly historical pedagogue.

His approach is at the farthermost extreme from the traditional rote-learning approaches, which, in my judgment, do little indeed to give students a historical sense. And it is this "sense" of history, the capacity to place ordinary situations into historical perspective, that strikes me as the most important and most teachable lesson we can convey in high-school history classes, especially in World History.

Beulah White: A Community Teacher for Humanities Classrooms
Jack Blodgett

Throughout the history of education we have learned to appreciate the difficulty of drawing a clear picture of exemplary education in the actions of teachers who have made profound differences in the lives of students. These teachers convey "community knowledge": experience and understanding unbound by any circumscription of student learning for which the teacher is programmatically accountable. What does it look like to "convey community knowledge" in the classroom? Have we learned at least enough to know that we cannot simply describe a model set of behaviors or components of a program as though the goal were mere replication by other teachers? We might focus instead on what the students are doing, irrespective of a teacher's particular method of facilitation, or of a teacher's particular "presence" in the classroom. Along those lines, we could propose a series of indicators of high quality learning, pointing, for instance to the list prepared by Martin Haberman in "The Pedagogy of Poverty Versus Good Teaching":

> Whenever students are involved with issues they regard as vital concerns, good teaching is going on. . . . Whenever students are involved with explanations of human differences, good teaching is going on. . . . Whenever students are involved in reflecting on their own lives and how they have come to believe and feel as they do, good teaching is going on. . . . "[1]

To the extent that it matters, however, that we learn better to notice, appreciate, nurture, and support the teaching dispositions that contribute the most toward the creation of exemplary learning environments, I propose that what truly distinguishes such teaching is the teacher's own manifest dedication to *being* what he or she would hope to help students discover in themselves: a reader, a writer, a historian, an ethnographer, a philosopher, an inventor, a citizen.

One such teacher is Beulah White, who, for three years, directed a REACH project at Beck Middle School in Georgetown, South Carolina. The project, called Pocket Communities: Recovering Hidden Lives, continues to evolve at Beck, contributing a conceptual framework for integrating the entire school curriculum. The original focus of project activities was local history, with the purpose of researching the individual histories and cultures of the several "pocket communities" that feed children into the consolidated schools in Georgetown. In his state-of-the-state address several years ago, Governor Carroll Campbell remembered Beulah's work at Beck and called her a "rising star in a new constellation of educational leaders in South Carolina." Beulah has since left teaching in the Georgetown School District and now works with REACH as an instructional coordinator in addition to serving as arts and education director of a community service organization located on Pawleys Island, near Georgetown.

Jack Blodgett has been the Executive Director of the REACH project for six years. For twenty years prior, he taught English in public high schools in New York, Connecticut, and South Carolina.

What follows is a series of pictures that aims to convey a larger portrait of what we might notice and appreciate in a teacher who would present both a mirror and a lens for her students' understanding within and beyond the artificial boundaries of a classroom curriculum. Most of the pictures are presented in the voice of Beulah White, with little provision of contextual information or interpretation according to a schema of educational precepts. The pictures are grouped merely into "Intentions" and "Texts." These statements, reflections, and exhibits are the evidence of good teaching: they have been selected for their suggestion of how a classroom can open itself to a community, and a community enter a classroom. The diversity of texts experienced by students and texts constructed by students all have a sense of purpose made meaningful through a connection with the life of the community that transcends academic parameters.

Some may argue that this series of texts depicts an atypical excellence that appears in some teachers quite apart from any opportunities for growth provided by an intervention project such as REACH. While it will always be true that some teachers attain a level of natural excellence without any significant help from, or even in spite of, the education system, one of the central tenants of REACH is that it is essential to raise public consciousness about the existence and importance of such excellence by shining bright lights on the work of inspired teachers to dissolve classroom/community boundaries. This work leads us to transform our entire educational system into a form that will nourish the growth and character of excellence, a form that will benefit students as they learn through their teacher's example to function within a whole school/community culture.

Intentions

1. It's tempting to use test scores as the deciding factor for our proposed project. That would be too easy. It would have no lasting value. The teachers of Beck Middle School know that we need to help our students become well-rounded individuals. Students must have an excellent grasp of their local history before they can comprehend events on the state, national, and international levels. In other words, before they can begin to understand the world and its chain of events they must first understand themselves.

2. Beck Middle School comprises children from many areas of the county. Some of the areas have quaint names such as Greentown and Graves Station, which has a section called the Village. Some of the areas reflect the influence of Native Americans, with names like Sampit and Santee. Still others live in recently developed neighborhoods called Kensington, Ringel Heights, and a former chicken farm transformed into Wedgefield. Many of these children welcome the harvest season by tromping through the Francis Marion forest with shotguns or gliding through the Pee Dee River system listening and waiting for ducks to appear. What better way to help our students improve their writing, reading, and sense of place and time skills than through a research project that spotlights their neighborhoods, their families, their churches, and their beliefs, customs, and traditions? What better way to encourage an awareness and appreciation for the uniqueness and to mir-

ror aspects of the areas than through this school-based project? Instinctively, we knew that the children could best learn about Georgetown by focusing on the historical development of individual communities. What were the special, quaint qualities of these communities? How have the communities changed?

3. Project REACH is designed not only to teach students about their history and the history of the surrounding areas. It's also designed to foster an appreciation for this history that will translate into students joining with others to become keepers of history.

Texts

From a project report.

Many of our successes are those intangible moments that never seem right when transferred to paper. Students read *The Secret of Gumbo Grove*, a book that gives a fictional, historical account of a little girl's struggle to save a cemetery in Horry County, South Carolina. It provided the perfect backdrop for the concept of "pocket communities." Included are letters the students sent to the author, Eleanora Tate.

From a letter from Eleanora Tate.

Dear Beulah,

I look forward to visiting with your students at Beck Middle School to answer questions. Rather than give a presentation, I'll come with lots of answers that I hope will be satisfactory to the many questions that your students will have in readiness. I'll read the letters, prepare answers, and give them back to you. You can give them back to the students after my visit. That way they'll have my oral answers as well as my written ones. Might be fun to compare, as I doubt I'll say the same things that I write down.

From a newspaper story about project events.

On November 5, White, along with teacher Debbie Long, conducted a workshop entitled "Developing Creative and Critical Thinking Skills Using *The Secret of Gumbo Grove* by Eleanora Tate." Students wrote reports on the book, describing events of each chapter. Children discussed each character with their teacher, who explained the history surrounding the southern novel. The reports were compiled in booklets that were designed by each student in a shape that represented something from the book. In addition to the reports, students made life-sized characters for the major characters. These reports and likenesses were presented at USC Coastal Carolina College's Children's Literature Across the Curriculum Conference.

Announcement in a flyer: "Stichin' Scraps . . . A Beginner's Class in Quilting."

Project REACH is pleased to sponsor a quilting class on Wednesdays from 4:30–6:00 PM beginning January 11 and continuing through February 15. Classes will be held in the Beck Middle School Library. The cost is ten dollars per person and the class will be limited to twenty students. Mrs. Carrie Coachman of Pawleys Island will be the instructor. Mrs. Coachman traveled extensively while her husband was in the Navy. Each new location added to her growing interest in local crafts. "Mrs. Coachman is a gifted quiltmaker. Some of her quilts have been on exhibition at the Rice Museum and others are on loan to the McKissick Museum in Columbia." (*The Sun News*) Plan to join us as we stitch scraps into memories. Each participant will leave with a finished piece and the knowledge needed to begin again.

From a news feature announcing Beulah White's presentation of tales in Gullah at a local cultural festival. Prior to teaching at Beck, White taught English as a second language to Gullah speakers on St. Helena Island while recording and transcribing her students' speech patterns.

White, a native of the Graves Station section of west Georgetown, is a language arts teacher at Beck Middle School. White grew up speaking the African-English blend and sees it as a cultural facet of lowcountry life worthy of preserving, even though she is aware of its limitations. "It's my baggage, but I don't open it all the time." Native speakers who want to make it in modern society have learned how to turn it off, White said, but they turn it back on when at home. Gullah has been preserved as an oral tradition and in print largely by white people because black people were reluctant to be heard speaking it, but this is changing, White said. But she says white folklorists have often missed the point. "Each person wanted to be an authority on Gullah and they didn't even consult with us." And the preservation of Gullah tales was sometimes done in a condescending manner, White also said. "If you are going to make a living off my people, then give them respect." She credits white historians and folklorists with keeping Gullah alive for those who weren't born speaking it, but pointed out it's not just a black language. "It's part of our history—and not only black history," she said. The same patterns and intonations can be heard from whites in the Charleston area and parts of Georgetown county. "Just listen," she said. "It's not quaint, it's part of us."

Classroom readings from Ladies With Hats, *a book of poems by Beulah White.*

Sing-Song Testimony

Ole Deek kin sho nuff testify.
Mama say she nebber kud understan
Wha he be talkin bout no how.

After wukin had all day long fer de city,
He wash up and cum to pray sarvice
All dress down,
Reddy ta praise de Lawd . . .

I . . . I jus lak to say day
I be yah to fa praise mah Masta.
Kn-o-o-ow sum pepil got de chance

Won take de chance.
Kn-o-o-ow sum pepil want de chance.
Ca-a-a-an gi-i-i-it de chance
Won use de chance.
Ti-i-i-nk Ga-a-a-awd I fa use mah cha-a-a-nce!

A Poem to the Old Man in the Picture . . .

To the Old Man in the picture . . .
I shall give you a name.
Only then can I talk with you,
I shall talk with you and myself.

You look like my grandfather.
You are a fisherman. He was a farmer.
You and he lived with the Land and the Water.
We called him "Buddy". I'll call you Mr. Mose.

I remember walking with him as he rubbed the soil between his palms
Did you test the water by smelling the air?
Did you attune your body to innate weather forecasts?
I'm sure you did.
Even now you soak in the air and sunlight as you repair your net.
Are you thinking about the day's fishing?
Or are you thinking about the land?

Mr. Mose, did you talk with your grandchildren about the sea and its mystery?
Did you tell them stories from the past?
Buddy talked with his grands.

He worked in the steel mills of Pittsburgh.
He made his money and left the furnaces of that city for the land he loved.
I wonder what he would say if he knew that Georgetown has been "blessed"
with its very own steel mill?
Did you work in a steel mill?

Mr. Mose, you're frozen in time.
Although you cannot answer me, I can always pretend that you do.

Old Man in the picture . . .
I gave you a name.
Then I talked with you.
I talked with you and myself.

From a news profile upon the publication of Ladies with Hats.

Her best responses to the book have come from children, her own and former students. "They look at me in a different light," White said. "It's been good for kids in the area to know that they can do it." One of the most interesting responses, White said, came from a child who didn't know there were any poets still alive until she read *Ladies with Hats*. All the writers and poets the child had learned about in school were dead.

From a press release advertising a community festival "From Scratch—A Celebration of Southern Food, Fellowship, and Fun."

What southerners call "spoon rations" will be on the menu at the first "From Scratch" food festival, slated for Saturday, March 25th in Georgetown's Historic District. The event, described by organizers as a "big church supper" will feature non-professional lowcountry cooks preparing a down-home menu including sweet potato pone, greens of all persuasions and more, for an expected lunchtime crowd of 1,500 Canadians and locals. Beulah White, who is coordinating the day with the Georgetown Chamber of Commerce, says that food has played a "tremendous role in shaping Southern culture. It is one of the ways in which we define who and what we are; a recipe is more than a collection of measurements. For the Southern cook, it is a keepsake, a symbol, an heirloom." White says that "From Scratch" will celebrate an artistic form of Southern cooking. . . .

From the February 1991 Educational Leadership *article "Assessment as Theatre: Staging an Exhibition" by Thomas Baron,[2] which describes an achievement fair that drew together ten of the original REACH school sites to share among themselves and a larger community the assorted evidence of the progress they had made.*

The REACH Exposition . . . fulfilled part of an overall assessment plan outlined by Archbald and Newmann (1989), the part they call "exhibitions": "Discrete competencies are usually assessed within the confines of schools. In contrast, exhibitions . . . involve productions of discourse, things, and performances for the public. Exhibitions also usually require integration of a broad range of competencies and considerable student initiative and responsibility in carrying out a project."[3]

The 1989 REACH Humanities Exposition was the brainchild of four teachers [Beulah White, Patricia Bradley, Debbie Long, and Linda Mathis] from Beck Middle School in Georgetown, who conceived, planned, coordinated, and hosted this first achievement fair. They invited representatives of the funding agencies, the State Department of Education, and the Office of the Governor, as well as university faculty, teachers, parents—and, of course, students—to attend. . . . The formats of the presentations—most led by students, a few by teachers—included dramatic productions, media presentations, and students reading their own stories and essays. Students from one school whose materials—and building—had been swept away in the storm surge [of Hurricane Hugo] had had to rewrite their stories about relatives: a grandfather and a 101-year-old great-grandmother, to name just two, had spoken of their lives and histories to members of succeeding generations. . . . In addition to the presentations, portfolio displays of student products were offered at several locations of the complex. The guests were encouraged to browse through the exhibits and peruse the booklets of stories, displays of poetry, and collections of essays that showed progress in students' expressive talents.

From Not Quite Prepared, *a publication of reminiscences written by the entire faculty and staff of Beck Middle School and used as a classroom text for student discussion and written responses. Its foreword states: "We, the members of the Project REACH team, were honored by their decision to share, with a large audience, memories from their past. These written experiences transcend all barriers." Beulah White writes in "Looking Back":*

Through the tunnel of time I look back and remember. . . .

. . . attending the very school where I now teach. I remember playing Red Rover and seeing little girls bedecked in white dresses wrapping a gigantic May-Pole. It was at J.B. Beck Elementary School I was given a sugar cube that contained the miracle drug certain to ward off polio. . . .

. . . spending my first night alone in our home. It felt delicious and I drank up the silence. . . .

. . . reading the *Autobiography of Malcolm X.* Traveling from New York, my sister Pauline bought the book to read during the long ride home. She graciously shared it with me. Unknowingly, she's started me on the path to reading "big books" containing 800–1,000 pages. Good bye Bobbsey Twins! Hello. *Little Women, Meridan,* and *Count of Monte Cristo!.* . . .

. . . competing in an oratorical contest before a jam-packed audience at Rosemary High School. A sister from Williamsburg County did "Thanatopsis" and wooed the audience. I took a deep breath and delivered my spiel about Goodness and Truth. She won 1st place. I won 2nd place and got my first check for the glorious amount of $10.00. . . .

. . . going to New York City for the first time. I kept reminding myself not to gawk at the skyscrapers because it would let people know, without a doubt, I was from the South. I got my first job working at Abraham and Strauss. New York was the most exciting, dirty, culturally diverse city I've ever visited. When the temperature dropped 50 degrees in August and the locals were saying how good it felt, I knew it was time for me to head South. . . .

. . . playing softball with the boys . . . jumping rope . . . peas porridge hot . . . peas porridge cold . . . conjugating verbs and diagramming sentences . . . flying through the air on the swing Daddy hung from the sycamore tree . . . fighting my brother, George, and destroying the cookie and candy jars in my mother's store . . . shaving my legs and wanting to cut my hair . . . singing in Howard High School's choir under the direction of Miss Pope . . . portraying Mary in the school's Christmas play . . . saying, "When I graduate I'm leaving Georgetown and I won't come back."

What distinguishes a REACH classroom from the kind we hope to help transform is the same as that which distinguishes the inspirations of such a teacher as Beulah White from the motivations of teachers who define and embrace their identity with reference solely to the values of an encapsulated system of schooling. Presenting before an audience of teachers attending a REACH conference, White states:

> As a teacher, writer, storyteller, and parent, my first objective is to educate, to foster personal, social, cultural, and intellectual growth. My second objective is to create a sustained interest in literature and to excite children to read and write, and read some more. My third is to teach children about other cultures through their literature, and my fourth is to use literature and drama as vehicles for addressing social and political issues. My stories come from living and contending with four colorful, imaginative, different children. My stories come from my daddy, my mama, my brothers and sisters, fire and brimstone preachers, folktales from around the world, children's literature, adult fiction, and my triumphant successes and colossal failures in life and in the classroom . . . .
>
> As teachers you are embarking on a journey. For some—you know the way; for others—you just caught the train harried and out of breath. Still others are waiting to be convinced. I'm reminded of the story about the farmer and the snail. It was a very dark night on a farmstead in Nebraska. The wife of the farmer took ill. Without any of the technology we take for granted available, the farmer told his wife that he would hitch up his horse and buggy and go the twenty miles to the nearest town to fetch the doctor. Well, the wife didn't want to be left alone and she begged him not to leave her. After he agreed to stay, he went outside on his porch and began pacing back and forth. A snail at the bottom of the steps inquired about his reason for being so visibly upset. The farmer told him the problem and asked him if he would go fetch the doctor. The snail agreed. Six weeks passed and the wife's condition worsened. Finally, after twelve weeks of suffering she died. Needless to say, the farmer was bitter and angry toward the snail. Two years passed, and, by chance, he came across the snail in his front yard. Without waiting for an explanation, he began to shout at the snail, who, looking bewildered and hurt by the farmer's verbal attack, then turned to him and said, "If you mess with me, I won't even go!"
>
> To those teachers and parents who are still waiting to be convinced, I challenge you to break down your old paradigms . . . . Let us look for and share stories with strong morals and values that teach customs and traditions, international understanding, cultural awareness, environmental awareness, tolerance, decision-making, creativity, and critical thinking . . . stories that foster a meaningful understanding of one's independence and interdependence in our society. Tales that are told and shared from one's heart make them come alive.

Creating Meaningful Change

The relevant research is already available to show that student success in education springs from a number of sources. In *Schooling in Isolated Communities*, Tom Gjelton enumerates some of these sources: trusting that all students can strengthen their use of language if helped to see purposeful opportunities for doing so; connecting what students learn to actual practice in the world they know; creating the occasions for students to take the initiative and to work together in teams as well as independently; understanding local history and the community's relationship to the world at large; experiencing the world outside the local community; and exploring the alternatives for future choices.[4] With basic skills on their way to their place on the shelf in the history of education reform, we now are preparing new strategies for effecting a higher quality of change in what students know and are able to do—including systemic initiatives that would align and coordinate all elements of the educational system with goals established by public consensus. While a systemic overhaul of the inconsistent policy structures currently in place in states and local districts is certainly appealing, the success of programs like REACH suggests that the greatest, most lasting change of all will be effected not through systemic reforms as such, however enlightened they may be by the evidence of research. Instead, meaningful change must come through the direct engagement of all of a community's human and cultural resources. Systemic reforms can too easily become programs that merely reflect the results of a shift in power that might supersede the priorities and individual identities of local communities and thicken the boundary between school and school learning on the one side and the community and community knowledge on the other side. The farmer's wife is dying and he is waiting for the snail to return with the doctor.

As mentioned early in this essay, many leading observers of REACH who applaud the teaching of individuals such as Beulah White would say that REACH has encouraged and supported teachers in drawing upon community resources to address the need to broaden students' horizons. REACH has worked with teachers to make up for the general deficit in cultural opportunities that schools confront as they try to educate all children. REACH has also worked to help articulate a community-wide sense of the humanities and the standards of excellence children should be able to attain and demonstrate. This particular way of envisioning our intentions is meant to suggest a question for those chiefly responsible for addressing issues of equity and quality assurance in providing for students who have at once the most to gain and the most to lose through their experiences in classrooms. It's an old question. Should the classroom merely reflect community standards and channel the community's resources toward enhancement of a teacher's instruction and a student's performance? Or should it be a place for holding those standards and resources up for appreciation by the light of dialogue, inquiry, confrontation with meaning discovered in ourselves and others? If it is more the latter, as we may affirm that our viability as a nation of thinking citizens depends upon it, and if the classroom and the community should not be forever locked into automatic opposition in the process, we need to recognize and to nurture, school-wide and faculty-wide, the qualities of reflectivity, generosity, originality, and daring—as we have seen in teachers who we can say are *of* the community.

Frank Smith makes the point that students learn whatever happens to be demonstrated in the classroom (or rather the learner's interpretation of the demonstration) through people, products, acts, and artifacts. "A teacher bored with what is taught demonstrates that what is taught is boring. A reading or writing workbook containing nonsensical exercises demonstrates that reading and writing can be nonsensical."[5] In the classes of such teachers as Beulah White, students are witnessing citizens who demonstrate the ability to negotiate confidently and thoughtfully the local and broader community's ways with words and actions while, as teachers, they go about the task of helping students construct their own informed interpretations of knowledge from experiences in the classroom within a broader community context of personal meaning. The authentic nature of interactions with such teachers lies at the heart of what we mean by the humanities in REACH and provides a center of essential activity that should inspire a transformation in the value structure underlying the nature and quality of what students experience in schools.

Our challenge, then, is not so much how to institute supporting structures for higher and more equitable performance and delivery standards for all students. Instead, it is how to help leaders in education and the community understand the character and commitment of teachers such as Beulah White—along with the nature of student activity in classrooms where there is a genuine basis for trust and an authentic connection to the wider world of meaning—in order for these qualities to be valued and supported in words and deeds of others who would then be disposed to join her in a larger constituency of teachers, students, parents, and community and educational policy leaders to understand before anything else:

> You never learn nothing if you don't
> go among other people. You's just keep
> on burnin up the chicken and makin
> hard biscuits cause you en eatin'
> nobody cookin' but your own.

> Beulah White, "Listening to Daddy" from *Ladies with Hats*

Notes

1. Martin Haberman, "The Pedagogy of Poverty Versus Good Teaching." *Phi Delta Kappen* (December 1991): 293–94.

2. Thomas Baron, "Assessment as Theatre: Staging an Exhibition." *Educational Leadership* (February 1991).

3. D. Archbald and F. Newmann, *Beyond Standardized Testing: Assessing Authentic Academic Achievement in the Secondary School.* Restin, Va.: National Association of Secondary School Principals, 1989.

4. Tom Gjelton, *Schooling in Isolated Communities.* Portland, Maine: North Haven Project, 1979.

5. Frank Smith, "Demonstrations, Engagement and Sensitivity: The Choice Between People and Programs." *Language Arts* Volume 58, No. 6 (September 1981): 665.

The Death of White Feather
Jane Christie

Grouped around a low table at the back of a busy fifth-grade classroom, a teacher, a historian, a CHART project director, and a student assessment consultant were engaged in a lively search for an appropriate assessment for a lesson on westward migration that they had developed collaboratively. They had just videotaped the first use of the lesson in a classroom. Discussion was animated as they considered how well students grasped point of view and stereotyping in both written and oral dialogues between Piute Indian Sarah Winnemucca and Oregon Trail pioneer Jesse Applegate; how closely the students had read the texts (memoirs of Sarah and Jesse); how accurate, yet imaginative, the student presentations had been; how "average" and "below average" students had shone; and how engaged and thoughtful the class had been as a whole.

Three ideas for ways to assess student learning took shape as they reviewed and discussed the videotape of the students: 1) provide students with additional first-person accounts of westward migration and ask them to comment based on their study of Sarah and Jesse; 2) ask students to listen to Buffy Sainte-Marie singing "My Country 'Tis of Thy People You're Dying" and write letters to her commenting on the song from the perspectives of both Sarah and Jesse; and 3) select passages on Native Americans and settlers from a textbook and ask students for a critical assessment based on their experience with the primary sources.

At this latter suggestion, the teacher rushed to the closet and brought out her fifth-grade U.S. history text, eager to share the chapter on the life of White Feather, an Iroquois youth whose days were filled with hunting and fishing. She indicated that he was a great favorite of her students and that she thought the text presented him in a sympathetic fashion, emphasizing the strength and vitality of his culture and suggesting that the students might profitably compare his life with Sarah's and Jesse's. At this point, her collaborators commented that White Feather was a composite, *not a real person*. The teacher was astounded. She had taught White Feather for years and never knew, never even imagined, he was in any way different from Sacajawea or any other historical figure.

Here then is the teaching moment—the moment when the teacher realized the limitations of the textbook. The assessment team was searching for an assessment activity that would encourage students to read history critically. What happened was that the teacher read one of her key texts critically for the first time! In this moment White Feather died.

The moment occurred spontaneously; it was not planned because the need for it was not recognized. It would not have happened without collaboration. The presence of the collaborative team made it possible for the teacher to question her prior assumptions

Jane Christie is the Connecticut Humanities Council's Assistant Director for Education. She directs the Council's granting programs in education and is a project director for the Connecticut Humanities Alliance, a collaborative educational reform project of the Connecticut Humanities Council and urban school systems in Hartford, New London, and Norwich.

about the truth of the textbook. Had she not felt comfortable in the collaborative situation, she could easily have hidden her confusion and would not have realized that implicit in the lesson was the ability to distinguish between a human being and an anthropological construct. If the teacher was limited only to the textbook, using a composite would be acceptable provided the teacher and the students were aware that it was a composite, not a real person. Since the object of this lesson was to encourage students to "act like historians," to use primary sources to gain access to real people, White Feather would not do. Presumably, if we had used the textbook as part of the assessment, students who had understood the lesson would have recognized that White Feather was not a real person. Historians do not study composites; they study real people.

As a result of the team effort in designing this lesson and its assessment, the teacher began to recognize that analytic skills employed by historians could also be taught to her students. These skills include the ability to read documents critically: analyzing, interpreting, comparing, and contrasting them; making judgments about the reliability of documents, finding their point of view; describing and interpreting historical materials in context; and constructing narratives from primary sources.

Central to the definition of quality emerging from this teaching moment is the surprise and pleasure that the learner experiences. Both were exhibited in the teacher's subsequent exclamation: "What were we doing with our textbooks all these years?" If for the moment we think of this collaborative team as teachers and student, we can recognize the surprise of the teacher who discovers, beyond the limits of the prescribed lesson, what was to be and can be taught. For the classroom teacher this is an opportunity to make more imaginative use of a broader range of resources, to cease reiterating someone else's information to students. In place of the old habits and materials is an emphasis on helping students construct meaning from the richness inherent in the texts, documents, and artifacts that chronicle human life and experience. Encouraging student creativity in thinking about the past does not mean making history up; instead it means fully embracing the open-endedness of genuine historical inquiry.

The Migration Curriculum Project

The teacher's fifth-grade class is one of forty-two Hartford Humanities Alliance fifth-grade classes currently piloting a new multicultural social studies curriculum that focuses on the theme of migration in U.S. history. This curriculum includes units on westward migration, African-American, European, Puerto Rican, and Asian migration. The Sarah Winnemucca/Jesse Applegate lesson, found in the westward migration unit, helps students recognize and understand stereotyping and use the methods of historical inquiry to study point of view.

The development of this curriculum is a result of ongoing collaboration among teachers, university faculty, and museum professionals funded by CHART and local philanthropies, under the joint sponsorship of the Connecticut Humanities Council and the Hartford Public Schools. This effort is designed to achieve educational change through curriculum reform that is *interdisciplinary* in nature, *focused in orientation* (abandoning the notion of "coverage" in favor of an in-depth consideration of a manageable number of important topics and themes), *directly relevant to the interests and backgrounds of the students served*, and *teacher-centered in construction and implementation*.

The Hartford Humanities Alliance recognized early on that social studies textbooks were inadequate for its needs because they lacked the multicultural perspective central to the new curriculum. The Sarah/Jesse lesson provided insights into the limitations of textbooks in use as well as in conceptualization. The migration curriculum introduces teachers to new ways of organizing knowledge that are informed by current scholarship in feminist, literary critical, and multicultural studies, among other fields. These approaches serve to open the existing historical narrative to voices undeveloped or underdeveloped in the past. Providing a critical understanding of how texts are put together is an important step in encouraging students to begin to think critically about this history. Historians do not often communicate these practices because they take them for granted as the working assumptions of their profession; they do not realize they need to remind teachers that the practice of history is the study of *real* people and *real* events, and that the historian owes the past as thorough and honest a study as possible.

In a multicultural curriculum trying to bring to the fore under-represented voices in history, we must let the voices of the past speak for themselves. White Feather presented a barrier through which the voices of Native Americans could not pass. Such generalizations reduce human experience to a stereotypical common denominator that tells us more about the group producing the generalizations than about the group being described. When the teacher discovered this serious deficiency in her textbook, she became less apprehensive about working without one and more committed to teaching from primary sources. The result for her students is that they now have more direct access to the past.

In the Sarah/Jesse lesson, they began to understand how historians work. They successfully read and absorbed material about pioneer and Indian life related in Sarah's and Jesse's memoirs and demonstrated it in historically accurate and sensitive oral "dialogues" between the two as well as in written work expressing their different points of view.

In the future, as the teacher uses primary sources to provide real voices from the past, she is not likely to dilute the students' sense of the past by confusing textbook generalizations with historians' attention to real people. Her work illustrates in microcosm how the migration curriculum encourages teachers to bring from the margins into the mainstream the many voices of our collective past.

As Hartford's curriculum and staff development director recently commented, "What many textbooks did in the name of multiculturalism was to color faces." Burying White Feather represents another approach to multiculturalism; it suggests that teachers and students explore the methodology of historical inquiry and requires listening to the authentic voices of both Native Americans and pioneers.

Acknowledgements

I am indebted for the idea for this article and many of its insights to the other members of the collaborative team whose work it describes: Connecticut Humanities Alliance Assessment Consultant Joan Baron and Project Evaluator Lou Ratté.

The First Step in Learning is Learning to Feel Good about Yourself
Patricia D. Bradford

I live and teach in a thriving city known to many as the nation's capital. To those of us who call it home, Washington, D.C., is a wonderful place to live. It is a city of diverse cultures with all the pluses and minuses of urban life in America. We are struggling here to educate our youngsters and to keep them healthy and safe.

Hine Junior High School is located in an upper-middle-class neighborhood of professional people, many of whom do not have school-age children. For this reason, our students come from outside the immediate school neighborhood. Most of our students live in apartments or public housing with a single parent and use public transportation to come to school. Our student population of more than 700 in grades seven through nine is predominately African American.

The needs of these students are the same as those of other young adolescents—to feel secure and safe, to be appreciated, and to learn and grow—but some also have to struggle with social and academic deficits common to students in urban settings today. To further address the needs of students in our school, we search for opportunities to make school a place where students want to spend time. To this end, the school climate is student-centered and one of pleasantness and flexibility to the extent possible.

The CHART initiative in Washington, D.C., which we call the Academy, with its focus on improving school attendance by changing the curriculum, was the ideal program for us to pursue. Three of our teachers applied to the program, received training, and designed a program tailored for our school. The training focused on the development of an Afrocentric curriculum, based on the premise that a curriculum that taught cultural heritage and pride would boost self-esteem and improve our students' chances for success. In our case this included studying the role of African Americans in the Civil War as well as looking closely at each student's heritage and identity.

In the 1990–91 school year, Mr. Vernon Jones and I team-taught a group of twenty-seven students for a two-hour block, five days a week. Mr. Jones is a science teacher and I teach English and Humanities. While we incorporated system-mandated objectives into our curriculum, we were not limited by grade level or discipline. We taught students from three grade levels in a multidisciplinary format and included learning experiences in communication skills, scientific research, art, music, drama, and social studies. We requested a longer class period and decided on a team-teaching approach so that there would always be opportunities for small- and whole-group instruction and interaction. This close working environment allowed for better teacher-student and student-to-student relationships, which fostered peer tutoring and unity.

Patricia Duncan Bradford teaches seventh- through ninth-grade English and Humanities at Hine Junior High School in Washington, D.C. She holds a B.S. from Tennessee State University. Before entering the teaching profession, Ms. Bradford spent thirteen years as a writer/editor for the federal government.

My experiences with the Academy helped me as a teacher because I was allowed to look at curriculum from the students' point of view and to formulate projects and learning activities based on students' needs, rather than on system-mandated skill requirements. I firmly believe that if learning is to occur, students must accept some responsibility for their own achievement and teachers must be actively involved in determining what needs to be taught and how best to do so. Developing the Academy allowed us that opportunity, and our school supported our proposal. We were pleased with the results, and so were our students.

We believe that even the most reluctant learner can be reached given the time and a commitment by everyone concerned, especially by the teachers who work daily to prepare students to be productive, responsible citizens. Young men and women who feel they are important and have a role to play in world events are the citizens we want and seek to develop.

While this sounds good, it is not an easy task. Teachers are realizing that what worked five, ten, or fifteen years ago in the classroom does not grab and hold students' attention today. We can no longer talk to, or at, children; we must show them and let them show us if they are to learn the skills they need to survive.

The twenty-seven students who participated in the Academy were referred to us by teachers, counselors, and school administrators because the students had problems working in the traditional classroom. They were students who had been absent from school a great deal. Some had poor grades and test scores to match. A few had behavioral problems, but some were referred to us strictly because of the Afrocentric curriculum and small class size.

Teaching students who for many reasons have had trouble in the traditional classroom was one of the greatest learning experiences of my life! I learned some valuable lessons that probably every teacher knows, but maybe we've been trying so hard to teach the basic reading, writing, and arithmetic skills that we've made the lessons bite-size when our students really needed larger portions. I learned from my students two realities:

- Students want to learn something important.
- Students want learning experiences that are relevant to their present lives.

Drill work is not important to students unless it reinforces something the students believe is important to them. Some of the class work we did involved drill work in mathematics, such as solving the Punnett Square to determine genetic traits using dominant and recessive gene codes. We found that copying from the board is not important unless the information is needed as part of a question the students are trying to answer. Memorization alone is not important to students unless there is an opportunity to showcase or use this newly gained knowledge. Lessons that students learn and retain for life must be important to them.

Now, how do you make reading and writing important to someone who does not like to read and does so infrequently? We did two things: (1) We read aloud daily and discussed our readings. (2) We read short pieces on subjects of interest to adolescents.

Reading aloud helped to improve skills and comprehension by involving all the students in the activity. Students sat in a circle and read one after another, a paragraph at a time. Vocabulary words were discovered, attacked, and written down from the readings.

Ideas and concerns found in the texts were discussed. We read poems by Langston Hughes—"I, Too, Sing America" and "I've Seen Rivers"; short stories by a local author; African myths; and fables from around the world. We read nonfiction as well, including an excerpt from the biography of Wilma Randolph, the Olympic runner who overcame polio as a child. We collected research materials on life-threatening diseases and social conditions such as poverty, drug addiction, and alcoholism. Each reading was personalized by questions like: Why is this important to you? What are the lessons learned from this reading? How could this have been avoided?

Sometimes the students were extremely vocal, other times they were baffled by the circumstances of the characters and events, but always they participated in reading, discussing, and writing about the issue or topic of the day. Admittedly, the writing was the hardest part at first. It seemed they could not, or would not, start in time to finish; many paragraphs were incomplete. But writing is a process, and it takes time to get started and to feel like you're up and running. Remember, these students had major hurdles to jump: they were poor spellers and therefore limited in the words they felt they could use, and they did not believe they had anything of great note to say.

Once the students realized I was not going to mark up their papers, that I was more interested in them "seeing it through" than in a perfect paper, their responses improved. I never allowed students to ball up paper or to throw away their drafts. Every piece of writing is an idea and ideas are valuable, therefore all drafts had to be stapled behind the finished piece. This gave value to their errors and took away some of the uncomfortable feelings associated with writing. As time went by, students would ask aloud how to spell words and even make requests for synonyms. This was great for them to be able to ask for help without fear or shame.

Mr. Jones and I decided that students who did not like school and who did not feel good about themselves might benefit first from a unit on personal history and heritage. We titled this unit Genealogy: Who Am I?

As the school year progressed, we found we never completed the unit. *Every* lesson could be personalized. When we studied the systems of the human body and nutrition, we talked about our body parts, our ailments, and those of our family members. We checked our diets and those of others we knew who were diabetic or suffering from drug abuse. As the students learned facts, they applied their knowledge to life situations that were important to them. As they shared family "skeletons" with their classmates, many fears about acceptance disappeared and bonds developed. Talking and working in pairs seemed to produce the best results. There were four or five students who liked to draw, and so it was natural that we made wall-size art of many things we talked about. Each lesson seemed to help the students answer the question Who Am I? in their eyes and in the eyes of others.

In the fall we read a short story titled "Letter to Ricky" by Jeff Postell, a Washington, D.C., writer. The story is narrated through a series of letters between brothers. We read the story aloud, with groups assigned to read each brother's part. We talked about the letters: the older brother felt responsible for the younger brother's incarceration. The younger brother assumed responsibility for his own actions and shortcomings. The story ends with the brothers' commitment to work to make things better for themselves and their family.

After reading the first half of the story, we asked our students to write about someone in their family who made a difference in their lives.

Time was allowed for students to write in class. Many of our students would not complete homework assignments. They had poor work habits and, as we all know, old habits are hard to break. Each person was required to complete the tasks assigned, and was excluded from the group discussion until prepared to participate. Since we were working in a team-teaching situation, Mr. Jones might continue with the prepared students while I worked with those who needed to catch up. Some students, because of poor or erratic attendance, were always catching up.

A student named Samuel Capies wrote about the person in his family he thought he most resembled.

> My mother's eyes are big and dark brown like mine. She and I eat alike. My father is 6'6". I think I am going to be tall like my father. I have 24 cousins in my family. I have one bad cousin. His name is Robert. We'll call him Rob.

Samuel's paragraph generated a great deal of lively discussion. For example: What do you mean by you and your mother eat alike? Why did you jump from one thing to another? First, you were talking about your eyes, then eating, then your father, then your cousins, and finally your bad cousin Rob. Why do you think he is bad? What happened in his family? Could things have been different for him? What would you have done if you had been in his shoes?

Students worked with one of the teachers and with their peers to edit and revise their writing. Spelling and punctuation were corrected only after all ideas had been added or expanded upon. Then the writing task was put aside and the reading of the story continued.

As we finished "Letter to Ricky," students were asked to choose sides. The lead question was, Did you feel it was Ricky's fault or his brother's? Discussion raged.

The next day's writing task was the topic Who Am I? Student responses varied that first day. As the year progressed, their writing became more detailed and reflective.

Note the progression of these installments on the same theme by Samuel Capies.

> September 13, 1990
> Who am I? I have three sisters. I am in the Linch Mob [*a local band*]. I have one brother. I have a girlfriend. I am in the band. I am in the 8th grade. I have one real girlfriend.

> October 3, 1990
> Who am I? I am a proud black kid who lives in Washington, D.C. I have three sisters and a brother. I am a young artist of Hine Junior High School. I am feeling good today. My name is Samuel Capies, but people . . . . . . [*Time ran out or student just did not complete writing.*]

> Late October 1990
> I am a unique, one-of-a-kind person who had a chance to be born. If I were not

born [*sic*], I would have missed school. I would have missed being a great artist, . . . my girlfriend. I am a good math student. I could not have met stars . . . [*This student met members of the Take 6 gospel singing group when they visited a local school.*]

June 7, 1991

About me, I am a loving person who likes to have fun, but not too much fun. I like to be different from other people. Different in a good way. I like to play in the band and I want to go to college . . . to Florida A. and M. I cannot wait for my birthday so I can have a car.

The writer is still jumping from one idea to another, but he is including more about himself, and his strong, positive self-image is evident. This sense of self-worth is essential to teaching if the experience is to be worthwhile to the student and if learning is indeed to occur. Through his writings, Samuel has moved from concentrating on who he is in his family to who he *is*: a musician, an artist, and a mathematician!

In general, people need to learn to evaluate their assets as well as their liabilities. I think sometimes in education we work too hard to simply improve test scores or we emphasize students' deficits, and as a result we overlook what students already know. Learning is more valuable to students if they have something to build on—a foundation of knowledge.

Exploring the Civil War

One specific area of knowledge about which our students generally need to know more is the American Civil War. The Civil War is not easy to teach because remnants of many of the causes of the war still exist in our society today. The Civil War may be glorified in some classrooms and skimmed over in others. Care must be taken by teachers to avoid presenting it as a "race war." African American students might feel embarrassed, hurt, or angered if the information is not carefully presented. On the other hand, these same students may want to disassociate themselves from the topic completely by saying that the Civil War is long over and has nothing to do with their lives today.

We believe much of the Civil War is missed by our students because it is not a comfortable part of our nation's history to discuss. An Afrocentric curriculum, such as ours, allowed us to study the historical events and to include those pertaining to African Americans, which are generally ignored. We asked questions like: What did the war mean to black people? How did the events around the war affect them and what did they do? What would you have done had you been living during the time of the Civil War?

We were fortunate to have Mr. Carrol Gibbs, a historian who specializes in the history of African Americans, visit our class. Through an educational partnership with the U.S. Department of Transportation (DOT), we have access to federal employees who volunteer to tutor, lecture, and befriend our students. Mr. Gibbs came to our class dressed in full Union uniform with his musket in tow. He showed the students actual bullets and the typical attire worn by the U.S. military during the days of civil strife we were studying. He also brought reproductions of documents from the National Archives that recorded slave trading, the selling prices of slaves, newspaper accounts of runaway slaves, and the rewards offered. He talked about the slave trade in Washington, D.C., in the very neighborhoods that my students knew. The students were completely unaware that their home city once had a slave marketplace, but the newspaper accounts described it in great detail.

We learned from Mr. Gibbs that blacks fought on both sides during the Civil War. He held the students spellbound for over an hour, allowing them to touch the musket, bullets, soda crackers, and other artifacts he described. The students stayed into their lunch hour to ask him additional questions.

We had done our homework prior to Mr. Gibbs's visit, though his information was still startling and eye-opening for some of the students. We went to the National Archives and learned how to research family records, census records, and military service documents. We toured an extensive photographic exhibit of the Washington, D.C., of old, bringing to life a time when many of the city's now busiest streets were farmlands with grazing cows. The archive docents also showed the students the Magna Carta and the Constitution of the United States. We read materials on the Civil War and the life of key figures such as President Abraham Lincoln. We studied the Gettysburg Address and watched again and again the movie *Glory*. We understood that black people played a part in shaping our country.

While students learned much information about the black and white abolitionists and the motives for the Civil War, it was interesting to note "who they became" when asked to imagine a day in their lives had they been alive during the Civil War. We compiled these short narratives and published them in an illustrated booklet.

Samuel Capies's description reads as follows:

> In 1861, the war began. I cried as my house caught fire as the soldiers marched up the hill. They marched up the hill where I used to pick the cotton. Uncle Tom called us together. I heard boom! Boom! I looked out the window and saw the blue from the north soldiers' uniforms. I heard them coming as poor Uncle Tom cried and cried. I saw the big green tree when it caught on fire.

This eighth-grader felt some of the pain and anguish that the men and women who were in bondage might have felt as they watched their only homes go up in flames. He chose to write from the standpoint of a slave who knew a famous, though fictitious, slave named Uncle Tom. Samuel seems to respect this character, but we are not told why Uncle Tom is crying. Is it out of happiness or sadness?

It is interesting to note that although all the students were African American, they did not limit their imagination by race or sex. Some of the students imagined themselves to be southerners, others were northerners, and yes, some were slaveholders, but they were good to their slaves! One young man even said he was Abraham Lincoln!

Of course, not all the students in the class responded as positively as those I've mentioned. Some continued to be absent from school and did not take part in all the activities, but the majority of the students did participate. Three students who had been in the special education program were mainstreamed completely into the traditional classes. Each of these three made the honor roll during the school year. Students asked to be part of the Academy the next school year despite our urging them to take other electives.

I believe our students learned a valuable lesson that perhaps even Jesse Jackson's speeches had not been able to convey. They learned *who* they were, personally and historically. Each one of them is someone very important! Now they are ready to continue learning important things!

The writing process movement of the past twenty-five years has broken tremendous ground in discovering ways in which writing could be used as an *active* teaching and learning process. In practical terms, students and teachers in many classrooms have been liberated from some of the mechanical obsessions and constraints that stifle students' natural creativity and inhibit the use of writing as a learning process, rather than exclusively as an outcome or a result. In theoretical or academic terms, writing has been linked with more formal issues of language acquisition and usage, and has opened doors to the use of writing and literature outside of the "normal" context of English, history or social studies classes.

The new freedom and respect the writing process enjoys has not come without accountability. One of the most obvious manifestations of this has been in the variety of techniques— particularly those involving the use of writing portfolios—developed to capture students' real achievements in writing, and the learning these achievements represent. We are in a difficult period of transition in the assessment of student learning in all areas, but especially in writing. The new assessment techniques built around writing portfolios requires tremendous investments of time and human energy from both teachers and students. As it evolves, assessment itself is has the potential to become more a part of the teaching and learning process, rather than merely an evaluation of results or the compilation of a particular body of school work. This has certainly been the case in the **Arts PROPEL** program, as Kathryn Howard's essay and the reflections by student Cara Rubinsky demonstrate. Arts PROPEL is designed to help students think artistically, and to help teachers learn how to document, measure and report to the community students' progress in the arts.

Similarly, as schools begin to focus attention on the needs of students who are not native English speakers, writing and literature become very powerful tools in a new context. One CHART program that focuses on language issues is the **Humanities Education, Research, and Language Development program (HERALD)**. This program is designed to improve students' oral and written English skills through a variety of teacher-originated humanities projects. Gilberto Sánchez describes a wonderfully collaborative course in which students from a wide variety of cultural backgrounds, with quite different levels of facility with the English language, find common ground in a learning experience based in theater. These students learn through creating, and create through their learning. The teachers are renewed through the process of designing new curricula, establishing the research procedures with which to assess the effectiveness of the new curricula, and identifying the methods for evaluating student achievement.

Illustration by Jeremy Schnorr.

Portfolio Culture In Pittsburgh
Kathryn Howard

A little white piece of paper, as expressive as the words written upon it might be, is not enough to express the true meaning of what Language Arts has become, not only to me, but I think to almost everyone in the class. It is a friendly environment of discussion and compatible argument, a place of freedom of the mind. A place where everyone, no matter where their talent lies, be it in writing, or music, or art, or even belly dancing, is welcome. A place to explore what the written word is and what it can be. A place to express the feelings deep within ourselves.

Cara Rubinsky, 1991, Writing Portfolio

These words characterize an English class in which students are free and challenged to become writers, critical thinkers about writing, and thoughtful assessors of their work. If these words were written by a curriculum specialist I would consider them. If they had been written by an expert in staff development I would respect them. Because they were written by an eighth-grade student in my class about my class, I cherish them.

The route Cara and other student writers chose to travel during the course of their language arts instruction last year became possible because of my own involvement in the Arts PROPEL project, an experience that enabled me to discover what I value about both teaching and the teaching of writing and to create a climate for students in which they could make similar discoveries about their own writing.

Arts PROPEL was a collaborative effort among Project Zero (a research adjunct of the Harvard University Graduate School of Education), the Educational Testing Service, and teachers and supervisors in the Pittsburgh Public Schools. Its purpose was to explore alternative methods of assessing student achievement in music, the visual arts, and imaginative writing. In this context, classroom teachers, researchers, and supervisors who made up the imaginative writing team met regularly to generate ideas for innovative ways to assess student writing; these ideas were then implemented in the classrooms of the participating teachers.

As these ideas were integrated into instruction, students and teachers essentially became co-discoverers, working together to identify and explore those strategies that most effectively improved the students' understanding and assessment of their writing and their writing growth. The results of the classroom implementation were then dis-

Kathryn Howard has been a Special Project Teacher specializing in Imaginative Writing in the Arts PROPEL program since 1989. She teaches eighth-grade Language Arts at the Reizenstein Middle School in Pittsburgh. Ms. Howard has a B.A. in English (Duquesne University) and an M.A.T. (University of Pittsburgh). Her publications include "Making the Writing Portfolio Real" in the *Quarterly of the National Writing Project*, Spring 1990.

cussed again, modified, and refined as the research continued. The goal of the participating groups was to incorporate the notions of more authentic writing assessment into districtwide curricula.

Central to the philosophy of Arts PROPEL was a theory of learning that emphasizes perception, production, and reflection. As we strove to make meaning of this theory in terms of real classroom instruction and equally real student learning, I soon gravitated toward the notion of using reflection as the key to change and progress. As we sat and read student work at our meetings, we often wondered what those students were thinking about as they wrote. As we grappled with the issue of what we valued about student writing, I wondered, as no doubt others did, what the students valued about their writing. Further, I wondered whether reluctant writers who paid the merest of lip service to the writing process valued anything at all about writing. As I considered these issues over time and spoke with other teachers, researchers, and supervisors about them, the answer became obvious. If we wondered what students were thinking about when they wrote, why not ask them? If we were truly interested in what decisions students made as they worked their way through the writing process, why not ask them to talk or write about these decisions? Why not make thinking about writing as important to students as the writing itself? Finally, and of greatest importance, if we were serious about finding *authentic* approaches to assessing student writing through a portfolio, why not raise the stakes for the student writers by making them part of the assessment team?

From these humble beginnings English and language arts classrooms have evolved into a "portfolio culture" that serves as the foundation upon which the teaching and assessment of writing is based. When we made a commitment to the writing portfolio, we determined that, above all, it would not be just another repository of writing to accompany the folders we already kept for each student. If we were to make the writing portfolio meaningful, we felt, then it must be a series of learning experiences for the student writers who would compile these portraits of themselves as writers.

The portfolio, therefore, would have to be embedded in a classroom culture that allowed students to make meaningful decisions about writing, that valued the choices student writers made, and that celebrated the accomplishments student writers achieved. The climate would have to be one that empowered students, teachers, and parents and other interested adult readers. Finally, this culture would engage student writers so that writing would become an intriguing challenge rather than a dreaded chore. In this context, then, the portfolio becomes the manifestation of thinking as well as writing. With the empowerment of students to make their own discriminating choices, the roles of teachers become less mechanical and more cooperative in nature as everyone becomes a member of the community of writers. Within this climate the increased writing does not result in more work for teachers; rather there is infinitely more satisfying work as students take on more responsibility.

The culture in my classroom about which Cara so eloquently wrote has evolved over the past several years with input from many contributors, not the least of which have been the students themselves. There are, however, several key components that have emerged as critical to the empowerment of student writers. One of these is a freedom to discuss issues central to writing and to literature-as-writing, an environment in which everyone's opinion is equally valid. This freedom to question and discuss establishes the members of the class as a community of learners and ultimately allows students to take risks without fear of ridicule or failure. Free and open discourse is really simply an extension of the common courtesy we all expect from one another, but teaching the processes associated with it takes time and much positive reinforcement. Many students are extremely reluctant to share their opinions because they have previously received either a negative response or no response, or because their lack of self-esteem as learners tells them that what they have to say is not important.

Discussions often start slowly in the beginning of the year until students adjust to their new power. In time, Cara's class and others like it eventually learned that as long as commentary is germane to the topic, it is welcomed. Eventually students talk directly to one another about writing and no one notices that I have removed myself from the conversation.

In my classroom, these discussions most often revolve around standards and criteria for good writing. The class continuously produces wall charts containing revisable lists of those qualities the students perceive to be essential to the creation of a good piece. Early in the year students place an emphasis on form, grammar, and spelling when formulating class lists. In time, as the emerging writers gradually come to place more emphasis on the *ideas* that drive their writing—after discussion, modeling, and making the reading-writing connection—the quality of these lists rises significantly. Often, then, these same students voluntarily move form-related criteria to positions of lesser importance on their lists.

These lists may be general or genre-specific; we use both in the course of an instructional year. The lists are important because they are student-generated and because they provide a foundation for personal standards and criteria for good writing as well as an internalized and personalized writer's vocabulary. These, in turn, empower students to make better decisions about their own writing.

While the classroom community of learners is considering the value of one another's opinions in discussion, a parallel learning experience is taking place with the sharing of writing. When Cara and her classmates came to eighth grade, these student writers had had some experience in sharing their final drafts of written pieces, but not in sharing rough drafts. In fact, students were quite reluctant to share drafts because of their fear of negative feedback. I tried to change this bias by writing along with the students, sharing my rough drafts with them, asking for their revision suggestions, and incorporating their suggestions into my own final draft, which I "published" for them. (This approach is particularly effective with less-skilled or reluctant writers, who have little or no idea what revision even looks like or how it can be used.) Ultimately, however, as barriers between students and groups of students were lowered, the writers began to see the value of sharing their rough drafts because they received practical and workable suggestions for revision from their classmates. Again, this happened gradually and after additional positive reinforcement, but it did happen, because the climate was supportive.

Cara is a wonderful example of just one kind of student who can prosper in this supportive climate. When Cara entered my class she had an excellent vocabulary and a strong personal collection of good models in writing; she was considered a voracious reader. By all traditional standards Cara would be considered an accomplished writer. Yet she had never thought about culling her own notions of criteria and standards of good writing from the models she read. She never sought wider audiences for her writing, nor did she define purposes. Certainly she had no identity as a writer, her ideas about revision and editing were confused and superficial, and she had never been encouraged to "think" about her writing. Finally, she had never considered her classmates as resources who could contribute to her own writing, but merely as competitors.

Thus, in her reflection on her year as a writer, when Cara writes about the decisions she and others made about sharing work, she documents a changing thought process as well as a changing personal practice.

> So none of us knew quite what to say when we first got into revision groups. It was easy to say that a piece was good, but now we had to give the specific "latitude and longitude" of the good parts. And how could we tactfully say that the ending needed to be changed? It was hard. The first time we got into groups to revise, no one wanted to make comments. We were afraid to write on one another's papers. But little by little, everyone began to feel more comfortable with each other. . . . We began to be less inhibited, we found ourselves not only able to write in the margins of people's papers, but we felt free to cross things out and write new ones in their place. We began trading papers, enlarging revision groups to make the maximum use of everybody's talent.
>
> Cara Rubinsky, 1991, Writing Portfolio

Cara herself explains the culture. Gradually, students find the comfort zone that allows them to concentrate on the tasks and decisions that are the core of the writing process. They are engaged, they are invested; this is the beginning of accomplishment. This is the reality of the PROPEL classroom.

Cara and I have both alluded to another central component of portfolio culture, an emphasis on the importance of revision. Before PROPEL, I had been often frustrated by write-it-and-forget-about-it writers, students who treated writing merely as an assignment to be completed with a minimum of inconvenience. In some classrooms—in fact, in my own classroom not that many years ago—the teacher often assumes the role of "error detector" and the student is never really asked to do any revision, but just to correct and recopy. Portfolio culture challenges students to think of writing as a sustained effort, to manipulate what they have written over and over until they are satisfied with the result. Sometimes, then, students write three and four drafts on their own initiative. They are rewarded in traditional ways for their effort, but their most significant satisfaction comes from having a finished piece that meets their own (and the class's) standards.

When students talk and think about the standards and criteria of good writing, they are reflecting. When students listen to or read the work of others and give or receive feedback, they are reflecting. When students revise, they are reflecting about choices they have made. When students take their writing folders home to be shared with parents or other readers, they reflect on the experience. They also absorb meaningful feedback about their writing from adults with a very vested interest. Because of this reflective nature of portfolio culture in Pittsburgh, it follows logically that our writing portfolios are as much an extended reflection as they are a compilation of work. In the end, all of portfolio culture is driven by reflection. While this is perhaps our primary contribution to the national discussion about portfolio assessment, it is also our greatest challenge.

The Process of Building a Portfolio Culture

Portfolios evolve in Pittsburgh classes using a natural progression. Early in the year, students are asked to respond in writing to simple reflective questions about each "process piece" of their writing. A process piece is defined as one that includes evidence of planning, multiple drafts, responses from other writers, and evidence of revision. It also includes any reflections that the writer him- or herself has written about the piece. Also early in the year, students are asked to respond to simple reflective questions about their writing habits. This inventory is placed in the writing portfolio. The process pieces become candidates for portfolio selection at a later time.

As the school year continues into the second semester and the portfolio becomes an entity separate from the writing folder, students have already begun to assess their own work through these reflective questions. Because of their participation in revision groups, they have already begun to assess the writing of others. Through countless discussions and equally countless class lists of the qualities observed in good writing, they have reflected upon standards and criteria for good writing. Thus they are ready for the more comprehensive, more thoughtful reflections that accompany each portfolio selection. They are also ready to view their writing as a body of work about which they can make discriminating choices. Students have a visible created product, their own text, from which they can work. The presence of this body of work is both an intellectual stimulus and a builder of self-esteem.

Students choose an "important" piece of writing, a "satisfying" piece, and an "unsatisfying" piece from their writing folder to place in their portfolio. In each case they are asked to justify their selection with an extended reflection. Later, they choose a "free pick" (no attached selection criteria) to complete their complement of writing selections. The reflection that accompanies this selection can tell the portfolio assessor how successfully the student writers have internalized the notion of the portfolio as a complete portrait of self as writer. For example, Cara writes in her free-pick reflection, "This piece is one that I think displays my growth as a writer over the past year. It includes a lot of dialogue, a writing style which I have not really explored in past pieces." Here is proof in Cara's own words that she views herself as a writer and that she is comfortable with and proud of that identity.

Finally, to complete the portfolio, students are asked to write a final reflection describing their thoughts about and experiences with their own writing over the course of the year. The extended quotations from Cara's work cited above have come from her final reflection. It is clear from these passages that Cara has thought about both her writing and the processes and strategies she employs when she writes. Cara's identity as a writer is loud, clear, and strong.

And so the legacy of Arts PROPEL in my classroom, and in many other classrooms in Pittsburgh, is at once both very simple and richly complex. In a simple sense, through Arts PROPEL we have established a foundation for portfolio assessment. In fact, we have implemented districtwide portfolio assessment in grades six through twelve as of

December 1991. Because of the unique nature of the Pittsburgh portfolio model, because it is neither a "best work" portfolio nor simply a repository for an arbitrary number of pieces of writing, we feel that the opportunities for teaching and learning can restructure our views of student writers in very meaningful and very positive ways. The clearest voice in the portfolio belongs to the student. The portfolio and the classroom culture in which it is produced provide the forum within which that voice can learn to speak with clarity, confidence, and understanding.

Acknowledgements:

The ideas and classroom practices discussed in this paper are the result of much work undertaken by many people. I wish to recognize the ongoing efforts of JoAnne Eresh, who keeps our eyes on our purpose, researchers from Harvard and ETS, and *especially* the supervisors and teachers who make up the PROPEL Imaginative Writing team. I honor them for their work; I thank them for their support.

Reflection on Writing
Cara Rubinsky

All right. This being the end of the year, I've decided to write a final reflection. Well, actually, I've decided that I'd *better* write it. It's due tomorrow. Anyway, I've learned a lot this year, especially about myself as a writer. I've learned to be a lot more confident about my work. I used to think of writing as an activity that I enjoyed, but I always hated the pieces I wrote. I've learned this year that a piece can almost never be characterized as either fabulous or horrible. In every horrible piece of writing, there's got to be at least one good part. The reflection (pink) sheets that we've filled out have really helped me to pick out good qualities in my own and other people's writing. They've also helped me to be more aware of what can be improved and what to look for during revision. That's really helpful. And I interpret this assignment as being a large reflection, but rather than reflecting on a specific piece, I'd like to reflect on the writing I've done this year in general.

Let's start at the beginning (that usually is the best place to start). I'd like to do kind of a quick little analysis of each piece. The first piece we wrote this year was an ending to Stockton's "The Lady or the Tiger?". I liked this piece at the beginning of the year, possibly because I really had no basis for comparison. Even now, when I think of how much I've grown this year as a writer, for me at that time, it was a pretty good piece. It helped me conquer my fear of reading my writing to the class. I've always been afraid of having my writing rejected, but this year I've learned how to share my pieces and how to react when others share theirs. After all, we are all in the same boat—and often times we're stranded.

Then it was on to October and on to longer, if not better, things. Or at least for me. That was fractured fairy-tale time. I liked my piece when I wrote it, but if I were to go back and revise it now, it would be a whole lot different. This was when I learned quite a bit about tact during revision. Even if you can't understand a piece, you can probably find something good to say about it. I couldn't understand a word of the piece I was revising, but not wanting to hurt my revision partner's feelings, I didn't tell him this. Plus, I didn't want to sound stupid. What if everyone else already knew what a necromancer was? Anyway, I'll talk more about that later.

In early November, we explored monologues. I had never written one before, and my first was a complete flop. I tried to write it in a German dialect. So what was the problem? Part of it was that I don't think I've heard anyone speak with a German dialect. Anyway, monologues were sort of interesting, but I find that it's a lot easier to hold an audience's attention when two or more characters participate in a conversation. My second monologue, also based on "The Last Leaf," was almost as bad as the first one. I still dislike it. I don't think that I captured the character's true essence, which is what I think a monologue should do. After that, I challenge you to find one example of a monologue in any of my pieces. I'll bet you have a hard time.

About the time of the never-ending monologue struggle, we were reading Saint-

Exupéry's adorable story, *The Little Prince*. My "Matters of Consequence" piece, which was the first to actually make an appearance in my portfolio, stemmed from this. When I first wrote it, I really liked the piece. I thought it was my best one thus far, and I chose it as my first portfolio piece because I thought it told a lot about me as a writer. Now that I look back, it tells a lot about me as a person, but doesn't reveal much of my true writing style. Plus, the grammar is not good at all. It's the kind of piece that, if you saw it in an English book, would tell you to circle and correct all of the mistakes. And it would take forever. Oh well. As the old saying goes, you can't grammatize 'em all. . . .

And you must remember the next piece. It went on and on and on and on and on and. . . . Now I bet it's coming back to you. Since you've probably read my "Biography of Almond Cave" I'll just give you a short little synopsis of my conflicting feelings about the "Almond Cave" piece itself. It was the first thing during this school year that I had actually hated. And I hated it with a passion. It was nine typed pages of absolutely nothing. Or so I thought at the time. Now I like it. A lot. The piece that I hated so vehemently won me a writing award from the National Council of Teachers of English. Go figure! Anyway, this piece taught me a lot about the proper use of dialogue to really enhance a piece and about the value of multiple revision partners.

And now it's January. Time for another free writing piece. This was one that I liked when I first wrote it, and one that I still like. It's about sheep. Now, you may ask "How could anyone write a story that makes any sense about *sheep?!?*" It was funny, okay? Here was where I learned that real life experiences can make a good fiction piece. If, that is, you twist them around a little bit. . . .

And then in blew March. And Golding's *Lord of the Flies*. And the ideas of theses (or however you say that you have more than one thesis). This continued through April. I hope I never have to write another expository paper. I hated the book and I hated the theses that I wrote. They were a heart-wrenching struggle (well, maybe that's a *little* bit of an exaggeration, but not much) and, by my own standards, a dismal failure.

Come May, we thankfully moved on to Edgar Allan Poe. I loved his work. I found him to be a captivating and absolutely fabulous author. I really enjoyed writing the Raven piece, especially since I love to write descriptively. I sometimes get very vivid pictures in my mind, and I love to try and describe them to an audience. What a relief. No more theses! (I'm *still* happy about that!)

And finally, June rolled around. And with it, *Animal Farm*. What a great book! This time, however, we had to teach a lesson about power through one of a variety of creative genres. You might not think that was so hard, after reading *Animal Farm*, but this time, we had to write before we read, a hard transition for those of us who were used to having at least an example to go by. But from my own personal point of view, it wasn't that difficult. At least not after I got an idea. That took awhile. This is a piece that I like now, but after a month or two, who knows? But even if I decide that I hate it next month, it was just one of the many ways of writing we've explored over the course of the past year.

All right. So I've taken you through the whole year (the abridged version). But I still haven't told you about revision, which I did say I'd talk more about later. At the beginning of the year, we really didn't have much experience with peer revision. Usually, our parents read our pieces, or maybe the occasional close friend, but revision usually consisted of running the spellchecker and proof-reading for grammatical errors. So none of us knew quite what to say when we first got into revision groups. It was easy to say that a piece was good, but now we had to give the specific "latitude and longitude" of the good parts? And how could we tactfully say that the ending needed to be changed? It was hard. The first time we got into groups to revise, no one wanted to make comments. We were afraid to write on one another's papers. But little by little, everyone began to feel more comfortable with each other. After switching revision partners for a few assignments, everyone sort of found their "niche" and at the same time found a partner on their level who could work constructively with them. We began to be less inhibited, we found ourselves not only able to write in the margins of people's papers, but we felt free to cross things out and write new ones in their place. We began trading papers, enlarging revision groups to make the maximum use of everybody's talent. And that's the best way to write. Or at least, we all think so.

And so I've taken you through it all. But not really. A little white piece of paper, as expressive as the words written upon it might be, is not enough to express the true meaning of what Language Arts has become, not only to me, but I think to almost everyone in the class. It is a friendly environment of discussion and compatible argument, a place of freedom of the mind. A place where everyone, no matter where their talent lies, be it in writing, or music, or art, or even belly dancing, is welcome. A place to explore what the written word is and what it can be. A place to express the feelings deep within ourselves.

Comments on "Portfolio Culture in Pittsburgh"
Howard Gardner

All too often, alas, schoolwork lacks either extrinsic or intrinsic meaning for students. On what one might term the *extrinsic* dimension, students do not perceive a link between the activities carried out in school and viable roles they might assume in the world beyond school. In this respect, today's students differ notably from youths engaged in traditional apprenticeships: the apprentice has occasion to observe daily the relationship between the projects to which he is contributing and the uses to which such work is put by the society as a whole. Not all schoolwork needs to relate to meaningful vocations, however. The classical myths that spellbind youngsters in early grades, the challenging mathematical puzzles posed by an enterprising teacher, the carefully wrought dioramas constructed as part of a unit on the pilgrims—these activities have, or at least can have, *intrinsic* worth for students.

When students live in an environment where literacy is highly valued and where it is mobilized productively every day, the extrinsic dimension of such activity is manifest. The Allan Blooms and William Bennetts of the world believe that such a milieu once existed in our country and that it must be recreated. Whether or not these agents of nostalgia are correct, it is clear that most students do not today live in environments where literacy is alive. Their parents may call for them to read and write, as a means of getting ahead in the world; but, all too often, the parents' own behaviors belie their message. Adult Americans read about one book a year, and there is reason to believe that American teachers read about the same number as their non-teaching contemporaries.

The attaining of intrinsic satisfaction from activities like reading or writing does not depend upon their importance in the "real world." Indeed, we know that individuals who have accomplished something in their lives gain a great deal of sustenance, self-actualization, or "flow" from their work; these individuals would become frustrated if they did not have the daily opportunity to immerse themselves in these absorbing activities. At the same time, however, we cannot assume that most youngsters will find it pleasurable to master the intricacies of script or of typing; that they will want to go through the steps of converting effortless speech into crafted writing; that they will crave the opportunity to rework drafts, suffer stinging critiques, or receive the letters of rejection that are the fate of every fledgling writer.

It is against this lackluster contemporary background that the achievements of Kathryn Howard and her students must be considered. For the most part Howard's students do

Howard Gardner is a psychologist. Trained in developmental psychology and neuropsychology, his research focuses on the development of human cognitive capacities, particularly those central to the arts. Dr. Gardner is professor of Education at Harvard University, and co-director of Project Zero at the Harvard University Graduate School of Education. He is the author of more than 300 books and articles. His most recent book is *The Unschooled Mind: How Children Think, How Schools Should Teach*, published in 1991 by Basic Books.

not come from backgrounds where literacy is evinced and valued; and they do not see themselves initially as becoming writers of any sort; in fact, given their view of writing as an unwelcome assignment to be dispensed with as rapidly as possible, and their own initial objections to collecting and reflecting activities, it seems clear that little intrinsic satisfaction has been gained in the past by most of these eighth-graders from these or other cognitive pursuits.

When successful educational innovations are described to burdened and defensive teachers, they tend to come up with one of two responses: "I'm already doing it" or "My students could never do that." Indeed, as Ellen Winner has pointed out, sometimes the same teachers (unknowingly) utter both rejoinders. Unfortunately, both reactions are equally unhelpful. The truth is that educational innovations differ from business-as-usual, but this novelty does not in itself ensure that they are impossible to implement.

During the Second World War, Winston Churchill promised his fellow countrymen nothing but "blood, toil, tears, and sweat." I do not think that the implementation of a program like Arts PROPEL bears a striking analogy to the waging of war against a formidable and ruthless foe, but the analogy is not entirely fanciful either. I was privileged to participate, from the beginning, in the Arts PROPEL project that Kathryn Howard describes and I can testify that there were formidable obstacles to its realization.

Arts PROPEL, an innovative approach to teaching and assessment in the arts, introduced a number of new and challenging demands upon educators. As the acronymous name indicates, students were expected to become involved in artistic activities as Producers, Perceivers, and Reflectors. They were expected to engage in writing activities on a very regular basis; to reflect orally and in writing upon their projects and their progress; to tackle specific problems in the writing domain (e.g., how to create effective opening dialogue in a play); to collect selected works in process portfolios. In addition, they were expected to participate actively in the assessment of their own work and in the work of peers; and to have their work reviewed regularly in terms of clear criteria in whose articulation they have participated. All of this stands in sharp contrast to most contemporary school districts, where writing is kept to a minimum, the focus falls on spelling and grammar, and no attempt is made to create the atmosphere of an atelier or a "portfolio culture."

To initiate and carry through a project like this is not easy in the current climate. Even well-administered big city school districts like Pittsburgh are subject to all of the pressures that beleaguer our nation today; and between the requirements for "coverage," mandated standardized tests, the often conflicting desires of teachers, parents, administrators, union members, and the general public, it is extremely difficult to launch any kind of innovative program, let alone see it through to a successful implementation.

As Kathryn Howard notes, Arts PROPEL was launched in a number of different art forms and in several different classrooms. It is also being attempted in other communities besides Pittsburgh. Success has been uneven. As an observer of these attempts over the last several years, I identify the following features as key to the success of such a program.

1. District support. Unless the leaders of the district go beyond mere lip-service support of a program, it is likely to prove too difficult to launch and sustain. In the case of Arts PROPEL, the program had the strong support of Dr. Richard Wallace, widely considered to be one of the outstanding urban superintendents in America. Under Dr.

Wallace's direction, considerable resources were directed toward the project. The resources included not only in-service time but also the long-term commitment of many of the most talented teachers and administrators in the district.

2. Time. From the start, teachers need time to meet with the program designers, with one another, with their students, to come to understand the innovative approach and to experiment with its varied implementations. Moreover, in nearly all cases, educational experiments take years, rather than weeks or months, to work. With respect to Arts PROPEL, it took teachers one or two years of regular meetings before they had worked on and worked through the major ideas; and one or two more years before they felt comfortable with the approach and ready to share it with their fellow teachers.

3. A niche for the program within the district's current mode of operation and future plans. Arts PROPEL was introduced into the regular English, music, and art classes. At the same time, it was seen as a major vehicle for the achievement of a number of district goals, including the introduction of alternative modes of assessment and the encouragement of critical and reflective thinking.

4. A means of demonstrating effectiveness. Though we live in a time where educational experimentation is encouraged, any architect who believes that her program can survive merely on the basis of testimony and anecdotes is mistaken. It is not necessary that effectiveness be demonstrated in terms of someone else's criteria; but the criteria to be invoked must be manifestly appropriate. In the case of Arts PROPEL, it would make little sense to look at the results of standardized tests. However, it does make sense to exhibit the work of students, to develop and make public the dimensions on which it is being assessed, and, most important, to secure the evaluations of individuals knowledgeable in the domain—in the present case, writers and teachers of writing.

5. Education of the community. No matter how well trained the teachers, how well conceived the curriculum, and how striking the student outcomes, a program will die unless it is seen as relevant and important by the community. Education of the community is everyone's job, from the classroom teacher to the union head to the major administrators. It involves taking time to show off the results of the work and allowing individuals to participate in the process of ownership. Strategic help from opinion leaders and the press can be invaluable.

Much of this discussion has a political sound, one that appears to leave the student work far behind, or at least pushed over to the side. On the face of it, that is unfortunate; one would like for a program—one that has already been singled out as exemplary in a number of quarters—to be able to be adopted widely and to speak for itself. Unfortunately, however, that is not the situation in America today. Even excellent programs are routinely dropped because they lose support of their constituencies; and many mediocre programs are deeply entrenched simply because they have a constituency and benefit from institutional lethargy.

As one of the designers of Arts PROPEL, I should leave the final evaluation of the program to more disinterested parties. The verdict will not be in for some time, because the program is new even in Pittsburgh and has barely been transported to other sites. From my vantage point, however, it is important that such programs survive and come to occupy a more central role in American public (and private) education today.

In the terms that I laid out above, Arts PROPEL has merits of both an intrinsic and extrinsic sort. Arts PROPEL does connect its work to roles (like a teacher) and activities (like publishing) that matter in the outside world; at the same time it cultivates in students a love of the written word and a pleasure in using one's own mind to reflect on what one has done, on what one's colleagues have done, and on how one might improve one's work in the future. In this respect, the sophisticated shoptalk and testimony of students like Cara Rubinsky serve as eloquent affirmations of how a once-burdensome undertaking can acquire personal meaning for young adolescents. If we are to have a population that is competent for the tasks of tomorrow, and one that gains enough sustenance from learning that it will continue to pursue learning even after the doors of school have shut, we must evolve programs that are meaningful for educators, for the wider community, and, not least, for students themselves.

Epigraph

CALIBAN   I must eat my dinner . . .
This island's mine, by Sycorax my mother,
Which thou tak'st from me: when thou cam'st first,
Thou strok'st me, and made much of me . . . wouldst give me
Water with berries in't; and teach me how
To name the bigger light, and how the less,
That burn by day and night: and then I loved thee,
And showed thee all the qualities o' th' isle,
The fresh springs, brine-pits, barren place and fertile.
Curst be I that did so! All the charms
Of Sycorax: toads, beetles, bats, light on you!
For I am all the subjects that you have,
Which first was mine own king: and here you sty me
In this hard rock, whiles you do keep from me
The rest o' th' island.

PROSPERO   Thou most lying slave,
Whom stripes may move, not kindness: I have used thee—
Filth as thou art!—with humane care, and lodged thee
In mine own cell, till thou didst seek to violate
The honour of my child.

CALIBAN.   Oh ho, O ho! would't had been done!
Thou didst prevent me—I had peopled else
This isle with Calibans.

MIRANDA   Abhorrèd slave,
Which any print of goodness will not take,
Being capable of an ill: I pitied thee,
Took pains to make thee speak, taught thee each hour
One thing or other: when thou didst not—savage!—
Know thine own meaning, but wouldst gabble like
A thing most brutish, I endowed thy purposes
With words that made them known. But thy vile race,
Though thou didst learn, had that in't which good natures
Could not abide to be with; therefore wast thou
Deservedly confined into this rock,
Who hadst deserved more than a prison.

CALIBAN.   You taught me language, and my profit on't
Is, I know how to curse: the red-plague rid you,
For learning me your language.

William Shakespeare, *The Tempest* Act 1, Scene 2

This Hard Rock
Gilberto Sánchez

My most recent playwriting experience involved a production called *This Hard Rock* developed in collaboration with the students of a drama course I taught at San Francisco's Newcomer High School between January and June of 1991. The play's title comes from one of Caliban's speeches in Act I, Scene II of *The Tempest* by William Shakespeare. In that scene, Caliban disputes the relevance and benefit of lessons he received as a result of the noblesse oblige of his European masters. His repudiation of the very language of his instruction prefigures the contemporary debate in American and European academia: whether curricula should consist of texts chosen mainly for their multiculturalism or those from the canon of classic work of the Western intellectual tradition. Ironically, Shakespeare, whose work is a staple of canonical reading lists, makes this issue one of the central concerns of his last play. I was struck by the similarities between the challenges of teaching and learning across cultures dramatized by Shakespeare nearly four hundred years ago and those I confront daily in my classroom—a microcosm of the ethnocultural hodgepodge known as San Francisco.

Newcomer High School, where I taught from 1987 until 1991, specializes in acculturating the most recently arrived immigrants to America. The students come predominantly from Asia and Latin America, although over the years the school has received representatives from most countries around the world. New students enroll at Newcomer throughout the school year and remain there for one semester, more or less. They receive intensive instruction in English as a Second Language (ESL), cultural/environmental orientation, and instruction in other academic subjects—often taught in their native languages. Upon completing this program, most are transferred to other, comprehensive, public high schools throughout the city.

While at Newcomer, I taught ESL, Social Studies in Spanish, and Drama—which I persuaded our principal to introduce as a curriculum elective in 1989. My interest in the subject grew out of my experience as an actor in San Francisco and a devotee of creative dramatic techniques developed by artists such as Joseph Chaikin and Viola Spolin. Before inaugurating my drama class, I had adapted many such performance techniques to teach ESL and Social Studies. Within the framework of the open enrollment I described above, my Drama class ranged in size from two students to a maximum of twenty-eight. I developed *This Hard Rock* with eight student actors: five girls and three boys, from Mexico, Russia, Taiwan, the Philippines, and Indonesia. Not only did the students speak different

Gilberto Sánchez has taught drama in the ninth through twelfth grades of the School of the Arts in San Francisco. He has a B.A. in Politics and Government from Ripon College, an M.A. from the Bread Loaf School of English, and is certified in Bilingual Education. He is currently serving a three-year term as a state of California mentor teacher. In 1991–92 he received a Bread Loaf/Clemson University Writers in the Schools project grant. Mr. Sánchez is on leave during the 1992–93 school year.

native languages, they ranged in English fluency from rank beginners to those who had studied the language for several years abroad. Eventually the production expanded to include a small orchestral ensemble from my ESL class and technical support provided by members of my Spanish Bilingual Social Studies class. The ensemble now totalled twenty-three with the addition of students from Hong Kong, El Salvador, Nicaragua, Peru, and Bolivia.

Imagine a teacher confronting such an array of cultures, languages, abilities, and needs in one classroom. Although Newcomer's students tend to be more heterogeneous than the populations of most schools, cultural diversity is becoming increasingly common, especially in America's urban public classrooms. No single textbook or standardized curriculum can remain pertinent for long given the continuously changing learning requirements of these groups.

At the same time, there are important skills to be gained by making the most of this seemingly impossible situation. Students and teachers alike are forced to abandon presumptions about what we have in common and assess each other more carefully regarding basic communication skills. Such assessment grows in sophistication as we measure ourselves and one another relative to cooperative projects involving an entire class. In drama we are concerned with a wide variety of very practical questions: Who can handle the most dialogue? How can we be certain each person will recognize his or her cues? What can each of us contribute to the show, other than language—art, music, dance, script writing, charisma? Which students work best with each other in any given scene? What assistance can we get from friends outside of our class, including other faculty members?

As my students and I would alternately lead, follow, speak, or listen—seeking answers to these questions—we shared an ongoing critical discourse. In a spirit of creative problem solving, we analyzed the progress of our work, which entailed evaluation and encouragement of each individual and of the group as a whole. At first the process tended to be rather messy, but crystallized as we prepared for performance. My appreciation of the cognitive and affective advantages of such cooperative, student-centered learning and interdisciplinary professional collaboration was deepened through involvement with the HERALD project. HERALD also confirmed my intuition that other subjects could be taught through theater.

Before my association with the HERALD project, I used predominantly conventional methods of teaching. I had the answers and designed learning activities for students to infer and recapitulate what I knew. This was a relatively challenging yet limited endeavor that presumed the superiority of my knowledge and point of view. Like a lion-tamer whipping his docile pride through so many flaming hoops, I prodded my students through exercises incorporating listening, speaking, reading, and writing. Come evaluation time, our little circus would be rewarded with accolades appropriate to our roles: laudatory recommendations, improved test scores, and competitive recognition.

So why argue with success? By 1988, after six years of teaching everything from beginning ESL for sixth-graders to Drama and History for gifted and talented seniors in high school, I began to feel that I was missing something. Neither changing schools nor moonlighting as an actor had been enough to completely relieve the monotony of my teaching responsibilities. I had always believed that my extracurricular theatrical experience enriched the life of my classroom. However, I felt discouraged from more active-ly using it in the courses the school district hired me to teach. Those courses included just about every subject but Drama, which budgetary limitations invariably relegated to the scrap heap of dispensibility, along with the rest of the arts. In addition, I had come to question my role as a teacher. I was trained to believe that the center of the classroom should be the teacher, using his or her training and experience to make contact with the student and the student's experience. But shifting state requirements, trends in educa-tional theory, and prescribed curricula left me wondering whether the students and their learning were still the primary focus of the education establishment in which I worked.

Maintaining a standardized curriculum in our increasingly heterogeneous society is a significant problem without quick or easy solutions. There simply aren't enough oppor-tunities for working teachers to develop new teaching methods and materials to address the diverse needs of contemporary classrooms. As I gained classroom experience, I want-ed to experiment with new ways to create a stimulating learning environment and mea-sure its effectiveness.

The HERALD project gave me a kind of permission to pursue these questions and to experiment with new ideas about effective teaching. The HERALD project encourages teachers to move away from didacticism, and instead equates teaching with teachers' own continuous research and learning. The key HERALD premise is that integrating content from the humanities with formal and informal research by teachers will improve stu-dents' language development. This premise resonated with my own experiences, reached after years of solitary practice and reflection. What a boost it was to discover that I was not alone in my preoccupations. They were shared by colleagues from throughout the school district, and by leading intellectuals like HERALD project mentor Shirley Brice Heath, with whom I was able to work during institutes and symposia. The com-bined intelligence and dedication of these collaborators energized our work and elevat-ed the level of our professional discourse.

The idea of teacher research is not a dry or abstract notion. We are encouraged to explore practical questions that arise in our classrooms, and to find solutions to problems or obstacles, not simply to note that the problems exist and quantify them. I was encour-aged to investigate and experiment with the published reports by educational researchers about the relationship between creative dramatics and what Professor Heath called "lit-erate behavior." The HERALD project enabled me to enroll in graduate courses at San Francisco State University and The Bread Loaf School of English. There I found valida-tion for beliefs and practices that had evolved primarily through a grueling process of trial and error. The work of scholars such as Dorothy Heathcote, Michael Chekhov, and James Moffett explained that creative dramatics is generally excluded from teacher prepa-ration in language arts because its effects are difficult to gauge on standardized tests. However, the information on which students *are* tested can be taught through theater arts—by challenging students to communicate with an audience through characters, action, settings, and plots.

Indeed, drama has proved extremely effective in teaching language arts skills in a vari-ety of situations. In a 1988 survey of research, Betty Jane Wagner[1] summarized the findings. Citing the work of Vitz with elementary-school-aged Southeast Asian immigrants, she concludes that drama contributes to a larger vocabulary and the use of more complex sentences. The research also demonstrates that in classrooms where theater arts are taught there is an increase in projective language (predicting story outcomes) and use of literate language in general (references to role, plot, setting, motive, and symbols). Additional benefits of applying theater in language arts include higher order understanding of language and symbolism; increased skill in narrative sequencing; enhanced word and story comprehension and recall; and improved understanding of cause and effect, motivation, and character psychology.

Despite such findings, most of the research literature I examined echoed the concerns expressed by Pamela Nelson that same year in *Language Arts*:

> Though drama offers these benefits, it has never truly been accepted as a viable part of our curriculum (Bolton, 1985). Classroom teachers have not received training in drama and have therefore hesitated to use it. How can classroom teachers and their students become involved in drama in a context which is supportive and yet meaningful?[2]

The question is answerable in part by examining the problems and objectives of language instruction in a multicultural environment. My research revealed striking compatibilities between the instructional objectives of ESL (listening, speaking, reading, writing) and the language skills students acquire through theater arts.

Much of a student's school experience is organized around relatively standard means of rote instruction, lecture, note-taking, and standardized tests. Many students find ways to succeed in learning through these methods, but many others do not. On of the questions I have found answered by the use of theater arts activities is that of how to reach students who have needs not served by "standard" instructional methods. Often, such students are more adept at manipulating concrete data than abstract information. This may be because of either their learning styles or an unfamiliarity with the language of instruction, as in the ESL classroom, where concrete examples make language comprehensible. In either case, the teacher must determine how to choose appropriate vocabulary. This problem is exacerbated when students don't share the teacher's cultural frame of reference—a growing phenomenon in American public secondary education.

One response to such challenges is the use of oral history in the classroom:

> The current emphasis on social history allows children to study the lives of ordinary people to whom they can relate. They study members of the community who filled the roles of parent, son or daughter, immigrant, entrepreneur, and problem solver. The focus is on individuals who were engaged in meeting their needs for food, clothing, shelter, association, and achievement within a society and culture. The important and meaningful details in the lives of these people are remembered because the children can weave them with events in their own lives. (Levstik, 1983)[3]

The opportunities for developing this exploration through drama are rich. By dramatizing personal and social history in the initial phases of language learning, students engage in literary discourse in an intelligible context. These activities are an extremely effective means by which teachers can help students acquire the language they need to survive outside as well as inside the classroom. Naturally, the students themselves are the best sources of that language, which can eventually be developed by contrast and comparison to the experiences of characters drawn from history and literature.

The HERALD project encouraged my students and me to put these theories and ideas into practice. Since the project placed a high priority on developing teacher-researchers in San Francisco, we participants were required to keep journals about our learning activities. In addition, we were asked to identify a specific question or area of concern to investigate in depth. We convened frequently in various forums to share our insights, successes, and frustrations. The process was like a roller coaster: alternately exhilarating and terrifying, but never dull.

In the summer of 1989 I wrote the following in my journal:

> It is important for teachers to learn more about the diverse cultural perspectives of our students. How can we tap them for insights into their impact on language learning and expression? My students are a treasure trove of original texts. They could be cultivated to promote self-reflection, esteem; inform American education about different ways of learning, adapting, creating; stimulate literate behavior and cultural appreciation.

My immediate problem was how to integrate these hypotheses into my teaching schedule. Most of us in San Francisco hit the ground running in September with two to four subjects to teach for an increasingly transient student population. Who has time to record research findings, above and beyond the demands of basic preparation? I feel fairly safe in suggesting that this was a problem shared by several HERALD participants. Nevertheless, motivated by the project's incentives for professional development and mutual support, those of us who took up the research challenge were rewarded by our discoveries, both theoretical and practical.

In my journal entry that summer, I appear to have been groping for a theatrical means to my students' social histories, native folklore, and cultural learning styles. Lacking formal training in anthropology, I familiarized myself with my students' cultural backgrounds through discussions and interviews to the extent that we could speak the same language: either English or Spanish. Since my drama class consisted of students from other language groups as well, I would try to recruit at least one student from the advanced ESL classes who spoke Chinese, Vietnamese, or Tagalog, and they would assist as translators. If such assistance was unavailable, we resorted to drawing and pantomime to communicate with one another.

At first we worked organically: I elicited their responses to images, stories, songs, and symbols representing such culturally suggestive phenomena as homes, national flags and maps, families, and immigration. A few days later we would transform these responses into tableaux of sound and movement, record them on videotape, and play them back to develop scripts for rehearsal and, ultimately, performance.

As we looked at the videotapes and drawings, I would suggest words, free-associating names and descriptions. Students who had some mastery of English would also contribute. In this way, we developed a preliminary script. We eventually wrote dialogue by adding people to these scenes, which were restructured to form our working script.

The cast found the process enjoyable and engaging, but exceedingly abstract. I found an almost poetic meaning in the words and images, but the students weren't understanding it on that level. This led me to adapt stories from texts such as Jane Yolen's *Favorite Folktales from around the World*. I would read a story in English and students would translate. We began to see similarities among cultures, and these stories led the students to memories and more concrete material.

As I observed the students comparing and contrasting international folklore, it occurred to me that I was neglecting references to my own multicultural perspective, which was emerging unconsciously nevertheless. I believe that teaching is learning, and I found support for taking risks in my teaching from my colleagues at HERALD, and from my own students. At the same time, I felt obliged to introduce the curriculum outlined in California's state *Visual and Performing Arts Framework*. The academic term would advance with or without us. What would we have to show for ourselves at the end of so much touchy-feely California process? This tension between innovation and structure was a constant challenge in my work with HERALD.

In order to help the students synthesize the theater arts material they were exploring in a way that would also draw out their language skills, we decided to develop an original multimedia performance work that would depict the evolution of theater in seven representative vignettes covering the development of Drama from its prehistoric origins to its more modern forms.

In selecting these vignettes, I wanted to give the students a sense of the breadth of dramatic styles, to include some material that would parallel their personal experiences, and that would highlight the similarities of certain rituals or performances across cultures. The selections included:

- A masked dance
- Rituals of birth, marriage, death, and afterlife
- A pantomime of *Oedipus Rex*
- Verses 93 through 110 from Act I, Scene V of *Romeo and Juliet*
- The song "Marat We're Poor" from *The Persecution and Assassination of Jean Paul Marat as Performed by the Inmates of the Asylum of Charenton under the Direction of the Marquis de Sade* by Peter Weiss
- The song "Somewhere" from *West Side Story*
- A rock-and-roll shadow dance interpretation of "Romeo Had Juliet" by Lou Reed

The masque, rituals, and pantomime were choreographed to contemporary and classic recordings of Afro-Cuban, Chinese, and Guatemalan music. Our enactment of *Romeo and Juliet* was punctuated by quasi-Elizabethan dancing to a live orchestral rendition of Thomas Morley's madrigals. A student actor from Russia played piano accompaniment for the group singing of "Marat We're Poor" and "Somewhere." Each vignette was complemented by slides illustrating the variety and universality of such human drama, including images of masks from a variety of cultures; paintings from Elizabethan England and the French Enlightenment; sacred pilgrimage sites of the world's most influential religions; and headlines of current events in our local newspaper.

The play addressed our collaboration in two ways. A slapstick pantomime concerned the struggle of teaching and learning about language and drama. For this vignette we used jazz compositions by Quincy Jones whose lyrics deal humorously with African American ethnic dialect and cross-generational ensemble building.[4] Second, we interspersed the vignettes with dialogue about the task of learning about drama in our particular class. We included our reflections on the content and process of our work, comparative multicultural perspectives on the various dramatic forms and stories, and correlations between our contemporary experiences and the historical contexts of the plays and rituals. Thus the production embodied another ongoing consideration of the HERALD project: the use of metacognitive self-evaluation. Our show became an expression of how we learned about learning and teaching drama.

No words can adequately capture the success of our undertaking, or how it felt to be there. No one was prepared, I think, for the significance and seriousness of our production. As a teacher, I was elated. We had found a way to unite drama, history and language, demonstrating what is possible when the disciplines come together. Fortunately, there are videotapes of some of our rehearsals and performances, but even these obscure the electrifying pride shared by the participants. At the end of the project, my students viewed the tapes and evaluated the production: what they had learned, and the quality of their contribution. They expressed unanimous enthusiasm in specific terms that exhibited the development of critical thinking, vocabulary, and self-direction. The following are representative examples of their comments:

> I realized that I had learned so much from performances like the history, the stories, the movements, the song, the dances, and we also learned English in that class. We learned how to handle our nerves in front of people, we learned how to arrange our breath. I think all of those stuff that I learned from that class and that project are really interesting and good.
>
> Jimmy Budihalim, Indonesia, Actor

> I have learned how to do the drama and play the instruments together with Eva, Josephine, Gary, Charlotte, and Joseph, made the song good and nice. From looking at the drama, I knew that people might be born again like the Buddhist said that people will born, then marry to each other, at last they died, and born again.
>
> Canice Au-Yeung, Hong Kong,
> Musician

> I really like this project. After this drama, I got a lot of experience that I could never get when I was in Taiwan. Especially I could play the *Romeo and Juliet*, which was known by everybody in the world . . . . It's really a interesting to know the people's feeling who is different from me. It's a challenge for me. It's exciting too. I really learned a lot from this project especially the history and customs from different countries.
>
> Eugenia Lin, Taiwan, Actress

> I learn how to act and how to dance. I learn about the *Romeo and Juliet*. When I am

in the Philippines I have no drama subject but in America I have a drama subject. I like drama subject because I learn how to speak loud and how to speak English.

Liezl Galura, the Philippines, Actress

Yo aprendí a trabajar en grupo, a combinarme con mis compañeros, a tener compañerismo. Yo estubo trabajando en los aparatos donde estaban los cuadros de representación. Por parte de eso aprendí mucho acerca de cultura como por ejemplo, la actuacíon que presentan en el drama "Diablera," como los pueblos subdesarrollados actuan con relacíon a sus costumbres.

Otra sería lo que presentaron en la atuación de las revolucíones mundiales y en fin aprendí bastante de historia.

Edwin Casco, El Salvador, Lighting Techician

[*I learned to work in a group, to interact with my classmates in good fellowship. I worked with the slide projectors. Through that I learned a lot about culture, for example in the "Diablera" dance how underdeveloped peoples present their customs.*

Another lesson was about revolution around the world and, in conclusion, I learned quite a bit about history.

Gilberto Sánchez, trans.]

Our work corroborated Wagner's conclusion that language skills can be developed through creative dramatics cited earlier. I would add that those claims were verified through our experience in other languages as well as in English. This learning/teaching process has also revealed that cooperative, multicultural interplay, directed toward the creation of a specific project, yields results that are infinitely greater than the sum of their parts. As students and teachers transcend presumptions and stereotypes about their roles, learning styles, and personal resources, they emerge as coequal agents in the enterprise of building responsible, literate behavior and appreciating the dynamic attributes of individual and universal cultural identity.

Notes

1. Betty Jane Wagner, "Research Currents: Does Classroom Drama Affect the Arts of Language?" *Language Arts*, 65, No. 1 (January 1988), pp. 46–55. Wagner also cites the work of Piaget and Vygotsky with respect to the advantages inherent in dramatic play and gesture in simulating cognitive development and decontextualized symbolic interpretation and expression.

2. Pamela A. Nelson, "Drama, Doorway to the Past," *Language Arts*, 65, No. 1 (January 1988), p. 22.

3. Ibid., p. 21.

4. We drew on cross-cultural material from many different sources. In addition to the jazz compositions, the students listened to the spoken introduction to "Wee B. Dooinit" by Mervyn Warren:

The Verb To Be

Please understand
We realize all these he be's, she be's
and we be's
Can cause the connoisseurs of speech
to get the heebie-jeebies
But after all if you don't be
And they don't be, who do?
So allow us to personify, and
Conjugate the verb to be for you . . .

© 1989 Back on the Block Music

Student Produced Play from the HERALD project
THIS HARD ROCK

[*Prelude: Ensemble Masked Dance, "Diablera"*]

DIANA: I love drama!

FLORENTINA: Yeah! Me too.

ROY: Well, I don't know. It can get pretty weird in there sometimes—like when the teacher asks us to act like animals.

ADELA: Look everybody—I'm a monkey!

JIMMY: And all those exercises! I swear—sometimes it's almost like P.E.

DIANA: Maybe—but then what about all that other stuff that we're learning in Drama, like history, and performance techniques.

ROY: Some of the plays that we saw and talked about *were* pretty interesting, if I *do* say so myself.

JIMMY: Like in *Oedipus Rex* when he gouges out his own eyes. [*Pretends to blind himself.*]

LIEZL: My favorite was *Romeo and Juliet*.

ROY: I guess it's OK after all. But then there's all of that ritual stuff. What is that all about?

JIMMY: Yeah—can you believe that Sánchez is gonna test us on all of that?

DIANA: You guys worry too much! In the first place, the big test is just to show vignettes representing the development of Drama from its prehistoric origins to its more modern forms.

ALL: Ugh!

EUGENIA: Fortunately, we don't have to write anything—just perform the scenes that we've practiced in class.

DIANA: *AND* in the second place, like Eugenia said, we've already rehearsed so much in class that the only way that anyone could fail would be to miss the final performance.

FLORENTINA: Eeeeee, but I'm afraid to do it in front of an audience.

ROY: Yeah—I'm a little scared, too.

JIMMY: Well, you remember what the teacher says about all of that, right?

ADELA: "Practice makes perfect."

LIEZL: That's right.

ROY: OK—let's do it. But where do we begin?

JIMMY: How about that ritual stuff that you were complaining about? It seems to me that since that's where all Drama began that we might as well start there.

FLORENTINA: Good idea!

DIANA: Well, what's everybody waiting for? Come on!

[*All perform rituals of birth, marriage, death, and afterlife.*]

ROY: So—that was a ritual, huh? It was kinda like being in church.

EUGENIA: I really like how, even though there are so many different cultures around the world, that we all celebrate passages of birth, marriage, and death through similar forms of ritual.

ADELA: So what should we rehearse next?

DIANA: *Oedipus Rex* is next on our time line. Around 500 B.C. Sophocles and the other ancient Greek playwrights introduced many themes and dramatic conventions used in western theater.

EUGENIA: That was over 2,000 years ago!

JIMMY: And wasn't it Aristotle who wrote *Poetics* to figure out the structure of tragedy?

ROY: A tragedy is like a sad story about when something terrible happens to somebody, right?

FLORENTINA: I think so—and *Oedipus* is pretty shocking.

LIEZL: Well let's get to it. Places everybody!

[*All perform mime of* Oedipus Rex.]

FLORENTINA: Ugh! *Oedipus Rex* is like my worst nightmare!

LIEZL: Yeah! As tragedies go I'll take *Romeo and Juliet* over *Oedipus* any day!

FLORENTINA: Me too!

ADELA: Why is that?

LIEZL: Oh I don't know. Probably because of the love story. I can really relate to it.

DIANA: I think that it's so funny that we can still identify with a story that William Shakespeare wrote nearly 500 years ago.

LIEZL: "Romeo, Romeo! Wherefore art thou, Romeo?"

JIMMY/ROY: We're waiting for you to rehearse the scene—hurry up!

[*All run off to perform the love scene from* Romeo and Juliet.]

ROY: Diana sure was right about all of the things that we can learn through Drama. I mean I've read about the Renaissance in my History class, but somehow I understand it better when I actually put myself in the place of somebody who lived at that time, like Romeo.

JIMMY: Yeah, I know what you mean. I remember studying stuff like the Enlightenment and the French Revolution of the 18th century and it all seemed pretty dry. But then when we learned that song from *Marat/Sade*, the Reign of Terror really came to life.

[*All sing "Marat We're Poor."*]

LIEZL: And in the Philippines—Cory Aquino.

EUGENIA: And in China—Mao Tse Tung.

FLORENTINA: And in Mexico . . .

ADELA: Miguel Hidalgo.

JIMMY: Yeah—it's kinda like Weiss, the modern playwright, was studying the present by turning it into the past. It helps us understand our own lives better.

ROY: It's a funny thing, but remember how in *West Side Story*, it was just the opposite? I mean how Laurents, Robbins, Bernstein, and Sondheim took *Romeo and Juliet*, a play from the past, and turned it into the present.

EUGENIA: You mean how Tony and Maria are really Romeo and Juliet, except living in America in the twentieth century.

ROY: Yeah.

LIEZL: And what a beautiful play it is! I think that I love *West Side Story* as much as *Romeo and Juliet*.

FLORENTINA: I love the music—Maestra.

[*All sing "Somewhere" from* West Side Story.]

EUGENIA: Well that about wraps it up.

ROY: What do you mean?

DIANA: She means we've just rehearsed the whole show that Mr. Sánchez expects us to perform for the school.

ROY: Hey, that wasn't so bad.

JIMMY: I think we should do it again. You know how picky the teacher can be. And besides, this is kind of fun—don't you think?

EVERYBODY: Yeah!

[*Finale: a rock-and-roll shadow dance to the song "Romeo Had Juliet" by Lou Reed.*]

Comments on "This Hard Rock": A Readiness Not to Explain
Shirley Brice Heath

In the British novel *Middlemarch*, the author, George Eliot, writes: "Let the wise be warned against too great readiness at explanation: it multiplies the sources of mistake, lengthening the sum for reckoners sure to go wrong."

It would be wonderful if education researchers and many in the public would follow Eliot's warning when regarding schools. Many of those outside classrooms stand ever ready to explain what is wrong with schools, teachers, students, and education in general. Thus they multiply "the sources of mistake" be setting up programs, policies, and procedures form outside or above the schools, teachers, and students.

The HERALD project of which Gilberto Sánchez writes embodied the spirit of Eliot's admonition and avoided "too great readiness at explanation" on the part of outsiders. From the beginning of the project, it was the *teachers* who chose the questions they wanted to answer about what was happening in their classrooms, the materials necessary to teach the units they felt their students needed, and the resources they believed important to their students. Those of us from nearby universities fortunate enough to work with HERALD teachers had all been public school teachers and remained closely connected to the everyday life of schools, where we found ourselves comfortably aligned with HERALD teachers as colleagues. We met not only in the classroom, but also outside of school on weekends and in the evenings to discuss literary texts and writings on education reform, as well as to hear what had been happening in classrooms with student learning and language development.

As Sánchez indicates, he and his teacher colleagues also chose the summer educational opportunities they believed would be most beneficial to their own development. At the end of each summer, the teachers met to share with one another what they had learned. Then they each went back to the classroom and applied their new knowledge, carrying through the year threads of texts, methods, and enthusiasm from their summer learning experiences. During the school year they held monthly seminars in which they discussed the problems they were encountering and the research they were doing in their own classrooms.

Throughout these learning efforts, the teachers also continually bargained, begged, and argued for common preparatory periods, some flexible alternatives to the standard

Shirley Brice Heath, professor of English and Linguistics at Stanford University, was instrumental in planning the original HERALD project and worked with Gilberto Sánchez and other HERALD teachers both at the Bread Loaf School of English and throughout the academic years in their schools. As a former public school teacher of English as a second language, she has a special affinity for working with bilingual students and helping them use drama, writing, oratory, and art projects to maintain their mother tongue while learning English. Dr. Heath is the author of a number of publications, including *Ways With Words: Language, Life, and Work in Communities and Classrooms*.

forty-five-minute class periods, and opportunities for departments with similar interests to meet with one another and talk. Again and again, such requests went to the top of the teachers' wish lists, and only occasionally did they succeed in obtaining any one of these requests. Hence, as the years wore on, more and more HERALD teachers reasoned that if the sorts of educational changes they believed possible for their students were to occur, teachers would have to work harder to bring about structural changes in the schools themselves and build new relationships between schools and central administrative offices.

Sánchez was one of those teachers who continued to try to bring innovation to his classroom while simultaneously working to help administrators see the benefits of giving teachers time to plan and work together during the school week. But teachers can struggle only so long to try to *create* a supportive school environment in which their students can learn, while at the same time trying to sustain their own visions of teaching. While faced with any possible escape from the double bind of being teacher and change agent in the classroom, *as well as* the initiator of restructuring efforts in the school and the district, a teacher may feel the need to seek a new location. Any such move is costly—in time, energy, and attachments— for all concerned—teachers, students, parents, and administrators. When good teachers are forced to move from school to school or from district to district in hope of bettering their own and their students' environment for learning, eduction suffers.

After many years at Newcomer High School, doing the work described in his essay, Sánchez moved in 1991–92 to another school in the district where an arts program promised to offer more opportunities for working in innovative ways with all students, including those who were not proficient in English. But schools-within-schools— whether arts schools or other special programs—are, more often than not, unable to escape the same kinds of administrative tussles and budget cutbacks the rest of the schools are facing. As the 1992–93 school year began, Sánchez and several other veteran arts teachers waited out their assignments; the arts program was moved to another school, and its future was unknown.

As the district struggled to control its budgets and shift resources, HERALD teachers in other schools saw their hard-won common preparatory periods ignored, as well as their long-sought common meeting times for departments with similar interests. Pockets of change remained, to be sure, and the HERALD teachers, like Sánchez, who had been with the project from its beginning, knew that many of the most significant kinds of changes the program had brought about would remain part of their teaching practice. The project had made clear a faith all too rare in school districts: individual teachers can make decisions about continuing their own learning and can help one another examine what is happening in their own and their students' learning. Moreover, thousands of students had experienced highly enriched language learning opportunities in their classrooms, and they would continue to carry their oral and written language uses through their academic careers.

In the initial years of the HERALD project, I spent many hours at Newcomer and in Sánchez's classrooms. Any time I entered his class, we both knew he expected me to act as a learner and as a resource and to treat his students as such. When his classes of mother-tongue Spanish students struggled to read English-language newspapers to prepare summaries for English broadcasts, I called upon my dormant ability to speak Spanish to talk to them about their interpretations. We met in small groups and worked on scripts. I listened as they sorted through unfamiliar vocabulary in news articles; they listened as I struggled to remember the English equivalents of Spanish words they used. When Sánchez's students were preparing to perform their plays before the entire school, I watched dress rehearsals that moved with precision and at a fast pace. After the performances the students gathered and I heard them do their own evaluations of how they thought the show had gone. I watched them fill their notebooks with recollections of their experiences in the shows, before the video camera, and in discussions with fellow students after the school performance.

His students wrote of what they had learned:

> I learned to work in a group to coordinate with my fellow students, to have a sense of companionship with them.

> I learn how to act and how to dance. . . . I like drama subject because I learn how to speak loud and how to speak English.

> I learned to be responsible with a group and to integrate and manage the sound equipment. I also learned that in cooperating with the group, I should never be late for practice.

What Sánchez enabled his students to learn went well beyond English. He orchestrated their learning environment in all his classes so that they carried the most important lesson with them wherever they went: never stop learning. The news articles read and scripted in class drew them to radio and television news shows in the evenings at home. His group work in classes enabled students to build and sustain helping relationships that went with them outside the classroom in their tough first year of adjustment to American schools. His insistence in class and at practices that students cooperate, be on time, speak loudly, be prepared, help one another, and assess their own learning progress carried through to their personal lives, even benefitting them in their after-school jobs—often working in the family business with their immigrant parents.

There are cynics who might argue that a teacher like Sánchez is "born, not made"—that he would have continued to do well with his students regardless of his participation in HERALD. Sánchez and other equally fine teachers would refute this claim, for they would argue that one of the most painful aspects of being a good, dedicated teacher is the fear of growing stale, of being content to return again and again to old strategies and to squelch enthusiasm, imagination, and invention in their own lives of learning. They know how easy it is to fall into patterns of blaming others when things to wrong and when continuing their own learning seems too much of an additional burden. What HERALD in its earliest years offered Sánchez and other teachers was the assurance that they could build on their intuitive strengths. Moreover, they could find learning experiences in summer programs that would let them know that numerous theories of learning, of organizational reform, and of language development reinforced both some of their established ways of teaching and argued for new and additional methods as well.

Eliot ends *Middlemarch* by having the narrator tell her readers that the novel's main character lived out her life achieving "no great name on the earth." But the narrator goes on to tell us something that could as well be said of teachers such as Sánchez: "The effect of [his] being on those around [him] was incalculably diffusive: for the growing good of the world is partly dependent on unhistoric acts. . . . " It is far less readiness at explanation and far more celebration of such "unhistoric acts" and "finely touched spirits" in teachers that the world needs. We need this celebration to stretch well beyond short-term projects funded by outside sources and to penetrate to the very heart of daily life within school districts and classrooms.

Descriptions of the Projects of the CHART Network

Over the past ten years, CHART has grown into a network of fourteen projects all focused on creating change and improvement in the teaching of the humanities. These projects take widely varied approaches to this work, but share some common beliefs and aspirations.

All CHART projects seek to renew and empower teachers as practicing scholars and as agents of change in their schools and communities; to make the classroom a more engaging place for students; to develop curricula and materials that will ask students to perform the real work of scholarship and inquiry; and to make the students' own lives and experiences a legitimate source of knowledge.

The following pages provide more specific descriptions of the origins and current activities of the fourteen CHART projects. Included is information on how to contact each program to obtain additional information.

Illustration by Keith Schmiedlin.

Arts PROPEL
Pittsburgh Public Schools

Arts PROPEL is designed to help students think artistically and to help teachers learn how to document, measure, and report to the community on students' progress in the arts. This involves:

- The *production* of works of visual art, music, and imaginative writing by students.
- The students' *perception* and appreciation of their own works of art and those of others.
- The students' *reflection* on their learning and assessment of their growth.

The Arts PROPEL Story

Since the early 1980s, the superintendent and the Board of Education of the Pittsburgh Public Schools have encouraged a series of major innovations in education practice. From 1986 to 1988 the district developed a critical thinking curriculum with support from the Rockefeller Foundation, followed by an invitation to researchers from Harvard Project Zero and the Educational Testing Service (ETS) to assist the district with a new approach to learning and to assessing student work in the arts. Based on Harvard professor Howard Gardner's theories about the importance of the arts as a way of thinking, Arts PROPEL encourages teachers to research and design curriculum projects, explore new ways of teaching the arts, and become "teacher-leaders." Since 1988, a group of teacher-leaders have worked with their colleagues throughout Pittsburgh's middle and high schools to help them restructure all arts and writing classrooms. This work results in classrooms where students generate their own knowledge and assessment of their work.

The Arts PROPEL Program

Teachers of middle- and high-school level English, music and the visual arts take part in staff development activities leading to the creation of projects in the various domains of the visual arts, music, and imaginative writing. The program seeks to transform classrooms from teacher-centered to student-centered, where the work of thinking through stages in the development of a work is guided by teachers but carried out by students. For example:

- Students engage in arts projects involving production, perception, and reflection of their own work and that of their peers.
- Students keep portfolios of their work, a process that follows the "footprints" of a piece of work over a period of time. Portfolios may contain sample projects, self-assessment, sketchbooks, notes, drafts, ideas for new work, personal statements, and audio- or videotapes.
- Committees of teachers and community representatives work with administrators

and researchers to analyze collections of student portfolios and to develop public reports on aggregate student progress in the arts.

• Portfolio assessment is being applied to other subject areas in the Pittsburgh Public Schools to increase academic achievement, attendance, and graduation rates.

Arts PROPEL Main Collaborators and Supporters

Phase I: 1988–91

Educational Testing Service	Pittsburgh School District
Harvard Project Zero	The Rockefeller Foundation

Phase II: 1991–present

PROPEL Phase II began in the fall of 1991. District leadership and PROPEL teachers and staff are now working within the context of the district to expand PROPEL to other content areas. This work builds on the Arts PROPEL effort, but is continuing without the collaboration and support of Harvard Project Zero and the Educational Testing Service.

For further information contact:

Dr. Judy Johnston, Acting Program Director
Arts PROPEL Program—Room 448
341 South Bellefield Avenue
Pittsburgh, PA 15213
Telephone: 412–622-3957
Fax: 412–622-3958

Advancing Teaching and Learning in Arkansas Schools (ATLAS)
School Districts of Rural Arkansas

ATLAS is designed to accomplish three specific objectives: (1) to strengthen rural teachers' knowledge of the histories, arts, literatures, religions, and traditions of the world; (2) to empower teams of teachers in the state's high schools to develop imaginative curricula and to promote professional development for other teachers; and (3) to promote collaboration among administrators, teachers, university faculty, international studies resources, and community leaders.

The ATLAS Story

In 1987, the Arkansas International Center (AIC), housed at the University of Arkansas at Little Rock, assisted in bringing about a legislative mandate requiring every high school in the state to offer Global Studies. The AIC approached the Rockefeller Foundation for support for a program that would help prepare rural teachers to introduce global arts and humanities into these courses and other parts of the curriculum.

The AIC gathered teachers, professors, and international resource people from around the state. They planned a program that would enable teachers from small rural schools to work in teams to design activities emphasizing reading and writing, connections across subjects, and interest in the cultures of distant parts of the world. In most schools, local business and community involvement has been key to support for international study in a state whose governor is committed to global links to inspire economic development. Students in several schools study a different country each month, celebrating its literature, history, arts, and customs. One school developed and sold an international cookbook, with the proceeds sent to help support an orphanage in Ethiopia of which the students had learned. For a state with many students and even teachers who have never traveled beyond their home counties, ATLAS has become a way to better understand America by exploring the world outside.

The state has approved a major school reform effort that supports ATLAS goals. Consistent statewide school restructuring plans will enable ATLAS schools to design whole new approaches to the organization of education. One district has already "block" scheduled its students so that two to three hours a day can be spent on interrelated study across the Humanities subjects. ATLAS has plans to reach out to all Arkansas school districts over a ten-year period.

The ATLAS Program

All ATLAS programs explore global education. They include:

• Summer institutes for teachers held in Arkansas that focus on the cultures of specific regions. In 1991, the topic was "The Culture of West Africa." In other years teachers have deepened their understanding of Central America, Mexico, and Japan.

• ATLAS has conducted annual study tours in Mexico, Guatemala, and Jamaica. In 1991 teachers studied in India and there are plans for a study program in Japan in 1992.

• The resource center at the University of Arkansas loans books, artifacts, films, and sample curricula to teachers throughout rural Arkansas.

• ATLAS provides access to Humanities scholars for curriculum development and classroom presentations through cooperative relationships with regional colleges and universities and links with other cultural institutions to support teaching, research, and curriculum development.

• Publications for teachers providing an information exchange and resource opportunities. These include publishing the ATLAS newsletter and collections of student work and teaching strategies, and dissemination of teacher-devised lesson plans. The widespread dissemination of such materials stimulates teachers' active creation of new classroom ideas. ATLAS reaches isolated rural teachers through its joint networking activities.

• One-day workshops, held regularly every year, dealing primarily with methods and strategies for teaching. Recent topics have included "Teaching about Africa," "Portfolio Assessment," and "Multicultural Education." Workshops on "The Heritage of Arkansas" are planned.

ATLAS Collaborators and Supporters

Arkansas Department of Education	Heifer Project International
Arkansas Governor's Office	Hot Springs Public Schools
Arkansas Humanities Council	Lee County Public Schools
Arkansas International Center	Little Rock Public Schools
Crossett Public Schools	National Endowment for the Humanities
Dardanelle Public Schools	Pine Bluff Public Schools
Fred Darragh Foundation	Rockefeller Foundation
Earle Public Schools	Russellville Public Schools
Eudora Public Schools	Stuttgart Public Schools
Fayetteville Public Schools	University of Arkansas at Little Rock
Flippin Public Schools	Winthrop Rockefeller Foundation
Fouke Public Schools	U.S. Department of Education
Fulbright Group Projects Abroad	U.S.-Japan Foundation

For further information contact:

Dr. Barbara Stanford, Director	2801 South University
The ATLAS Project	Little Rock, AR 72204
Arkansas International Center	Telephone: 501-569-3282
University of Arkansas at Little Rock	FAX: 501-569-8538

Connecticut Humanities Alliance
Hartford, New London, and Norwich, Connecticut Schools

The **CONNECTICUT HUMANITIES ALLIANCE** strives to: (1) promote innovative approaches to Humanities teaching and learning in Connecticut's urban schools; (2) build lasting alliances between urban school systems, universities, museums, and other cultural institutions and philanthropies; and (3) seek significant educational change at the local level through interdisciplinary curricula created by teachers working collaboratively and connecting school study with the cultures of diverse students.

The CONNECTICUT HUMANITIES ALLIANCE Story

The statewide Connecticut Humanities Council created a major program to assist museums in strengthening their capacity to serve teachers and schools. Short institutes and workshops encouraged institutions to make their historical and artistic resources more available to teachers. In 1989, the Rockefeller Foundation provided the Connecticut Humanities Council with a planning grant to begin to consider ways in which its groundwork with museums and teachers could be developed to generate systemic change in troubled urban schools. Planning with teachers, professors, and curators resulted in collaborative efforts in three Connecticut cities to change the way history is taught. School administrators support the planning process, and cultural institutions provide access to primary resources for teaching about the histories of all the people who have lived and worked in the state.

The CONNECTICUT HUMANITIES ALLIANCE hopes to build on its growing relationship with the Connecticut State Department of Education's innovative performance assessment program and a major new urban education initiative. The Connecticut Humanities Council hopes the new curricula will engage students more actively in school and community throughout the state.

CONNECTICUT HUMANITIES ALLIANCE Programs

Hartford fourth- and fifth-grade teachers are revising the American History curriculum to introduce the contributions of diverse people to state and national history through the themes of local history and migration.

Hartford sixth-grade teachers are constructing a World History curriculum focusing on cities as windows into world cultures. These curricula are now being piloted in twenty-seven elementary schools. Teachers study new historical material in summer institutes and in guided programs in museums and historical societies, jointly developing new approaches to history for implementation throughout the school district.

In New London and Norwich ninth-grade Social Studies, English, Art, and Music teachers attended two-week institutes in the summers of 1990 and 1991. They are working to integrate Social Studies, English, Art, and Music into a single, interdisciplinary

"World History, Language and Culture" curriculum for system-wide implementation in 1992–93. Local colleges, arts organizations, and historical institutions collaborate with teachers in their work.

CONNECTICUT HUMANITIES ALLIANCE
Collaborators and Supporters

Aetna Foundation
Connecticut College
Connecticut Historical Society
Connecticut State Department of
  Education
Hartford Foundation in Public Giving
Hartford Public Schools
Hill-Stead Museum
Lyman Allyn Art Museum
Mark Twain Memorial
Mystic Seaport Museum
New London Public Schools
Norwich Free Academy
Old Sturbridge Village
The Rockefeller Foundation
St. Joseph's College
Slater Memorial Museum
The Travelers Companies
Trinity College
U.S. Coast Guard Academy
University of Hartford
Wadsworth Atheneum

For further information contact:

Ms. Jane Christie, Assistant Director for Education
Connecticut Humanities Council
41 Lawn Avenue
Middletown, CT 06459–0185
Telephone: 203–347–6888
Fax: 203–347–0783

Curriculum for Restructuring Education and New Teaching Strategies (CURRENTS)
New Mexico Public School Districts—Statewide

The New Mexico **CURRENTS** program is an effort of the Albuquerque-based Hispanic Culture Foundation to provide teams of educators in restructuring elementary and secondary school with culturally relevant arts and humanities content, institutional support, and technical assistance in curriculum development and methodology. Its goal is to empower teachers to prepare New Mexico's children to function more effectively in their rich multicultural environment, while developing models that can be adopted by individual schools and districts statewide, and used to provide teacher enhancement and foster systemic change. Collaboration is being built with local, state, and national institutions and resources.

The CURRENTS Story

Sixty percent of New Mexico's school-aged population are minority students. In spite of a rich and multifaceted heritage in the humanities and the arts, extending back at least five hundred years, the vast majority of Hispanic, Native American, and other children are culturally illiterate. To date, there have been few programs that address cultural literacy or utilize culturally relevant humanities and arts teaching to provide these students with a base for enhanced critical learning.

The Hispanic Culture Foundation was funded by the National Endowment for the Humanities in 1989 to provide a statewide summer institute for teachers that focused on Hispanic culture. With further support from the Rockefeller Foundation, the Hispanic Culture Foundation expanded its work into a project serving teams of teachers from elementary and secondary schools throughout the state, with a goal of creating substantial change in school curricula to accommodate New Mexico's multicultural heritage. The state's support of restructuring schools has also enabled teachers to conduct this curriculum development within the context of broad school reform. Seven schools participated in the first year of the program, integrating their new arts and humanities knowledge into curricula that included studying the architecture of New Mexico's Hispanic villages and Native American pueblos; exploring and interpreting seasonal festivals within the Hispanic, Native American, Anglo American, and African American traditions; helping students learn to read and write through poetry, legends, storytelling, oral history, and visual arts.

Four more schools were added in the second year of the program, and additional support was received from the Kellogg Foundation. As the program entered its third year, the New Mexico State Department of Education provided support for the development of curricular materials that can be used by schools statewide.

CURRENTS Programs

Professional Development for School Teams

• Two- and three-week residential summer institutes. In 1991 the topic focused on "Understanding Cross-Cultural Exchange and Development Through Ethnohistory and Literature." In 1992 the institute had four components: (1) Studies in the Humanities; (2) Iconography: Writing from within Culture; (3) Multicultural and Arts Integration of Curricula; and (4) "Pajarito: A Community Oral History Project."

• Quarterly symposia throughout the school year on topics from New Mexico's multicultural arts and humanities. These topics have included the development of Northern New Mexico Hispanic villages; the Southern New Mexico perspective; storytelling as a means to cross-cultural understanding; and the use of literature in developing multicultural, interactive lessons for the classroom.

Grants Program

• Small grants for teacher development, materials, honoraria for guest presenters, and other direct costs of each school's project are made on an annual basis.

Support Services

• On-site assistance is provided in project development and implementation. Identification and links with resources and collaborators in the humanities and arts are provided to the schools; materials from the Hispanic Culture Foundation's resource library, including textbooks, videos, bibliographies, and research materials, are available on loan to schools throughout the state.

School Projects

• All school in the CURRENTS program implement a common theme, "Streams of History: Our School, Our Community, Ourselves," through a curriculum that fits the unique characteristics of each school and its community. While the approaches to these projects are diverse, all are team-planned, using interdisciplinary approaches or working across grade levels or in clusters. The teachers serve as facilitators for students who research and write about their schools, their communities, their families, and the world. Project range form local to world history, journal-writing to comparative literature, language arts to English as a second language, geography to natural sciences and regional architecture. In each of these project the schools collaborate with local scholars and artists, institutions of higher education, historical societies, museums, newspapers, churches and other archival collections.

CURRENTS Collaborators and Supporters

Albuquerque Public Schools
Anixter Foundation
Archdiocese of Santa Fe
Bureau of Indian Affairs/Taos Pueblo
Cobre Consolidated Schools
College of Santa Fe
The William Randolph Hearst
  Foundation
The W. K. Kellogg Foundation
La Posada de Albuquerque
Las Cruces Public Schools
Las Vegas City Public Schools
Los Lunas Public Schools
Museum of New Mexico
  Division of Educational Services
  Museum of Indian Art and Culture
  Musuem of International Folk Art

Palace of the Governors
New Mexico Highlands University
New Mexico Museum of Natural History
New Mexico State Department
  of Education
Old Cienega Village Musuem
Panasonic Foundation
Re:Learning New Mexico
The Rockefeller Foundation
Santa Fe Public Schools
Storytellers International
Taos Public Schools
The University of New Mexico
  Center for Southwest Research
  College of Education
  Latin American Institute
  Maxwell Musuem of Anthropology

For further information contact:

Dr. A. Gabriel Meléndez, Executive Director
Ms. Reeve Love, Coordinator of Educational Programs
Hispanic Culture Foundation
P.O. Box 7279
Albuquerque, NM 87194
Telephone: 505–831-8360
FAX: 505–831-8365

Humanities Education, Research, and Language Development
(HERALD)
San Francisco Public Schools

HERALD seeks to improve students' oral and written English in the high schools of San Francisco, where sixty-four percent of students have limited English proficiency.

The HERALD Story

San Francisco's classrooms are packed with students speaking scores of languages. The superintendent of schools saw a major need to help these students improve their English skills and turned to the San Francisco Education Fund to assist in developing a program to address this. Researchers in the cultural contexts of language, and particularly Stanford University Professor Shirley Brice Heath, worked with the San Francisco Education Fund to assist administrators and teachers in developing student-centered classrooms. Teachers also worked with other leaders in language and writing at the Bread Loaf School of English and at the University of California at Berkeley. Through such guidance, teachers have reorganized classrooms so that students have greatly increased opportunities to use oral and written language, to interact with peers, and to work cooperatively, thereby gaining greater power of expression. Teacher "inquiry," or research, allows teachers to study their own teaching methods and their effects on students' language learning. One teacher has changed from doing most of the talking in his class to helping students themselves use language more extensively in order to solve problems requiring group interactions. In another school, a large team of teachers observe one another's classrooms and plan interactive curricula. The district hopes to incorporate HERALD teaching approaches into an increasing number of high-school classrooms over the next three years.

HERALD Programs

• Teachers from each of San Francisco's high schools form interdisciplinary teams to study ways of increasing students' opportunities to use language and to design new teaching approaches for classrooms that encourage student-centered learning.

• Teachers conduct research into the effects of new teaching approaches in their classrooms with the goal of improving students' language use.

• Grants to school teams provide books, speakers and performers, video cameras, field trips, and other resources for a variety of activities for individual teachers and teams to enhance language usage.

• LIVE Summer School and the districtwide speech tournament involve students in special opportunities to share their learning with one another and the public across a wide range of academic and cultural backgrounds.

HERALD Collaborators and Supporters

The Rockefeller Foundation
San Francisco Foundation
San Francisco Unified School District
The Stuart Foundations

San Francisco Arts Project
San Francisco Education Fund
Strategies for Media Literacy, Inc.

For further information contact:

Ms. Ruth Schoenbach, Project Director
The HERALD Project
Parkside Center
2550 - 25th Avenue
San Francisco, CA 94116
Telephone: 415–566-0230
Fax: 415–241-6283

HUMANITAS
Los Angeles Unified School District

HUMANITAS strengthens the teaching of humanities in Los Angeles public high schools through teacher-directed, interdisciplinary, thematic instruction, with an emphasis on multicultural subject matter. Currently three or four teachers per grade level coordinate instruction in history, English, art, social studies, mathematics, or science in each of thirty-six high schools.

The HUMANITAS Story

In the early 1980s, a team of teachers in a magnet program for the humanities had created a team-taught, thematically organized, interdisciplinary humanities program. Students in the program were reading and writing on sophisticated topics, gaining access to major philosophical writers, and learning together how to question, probe, and fine-tune their own ideas. Recognizing that such learning could happen for all young people of average ability, the Los Angeles Educational Partnership developed a program to replicate it in schools all over the district. With an emphasis on reading historical and philosophical writing rather than textbooks, and a grounding in frequent student writing and cooperative learning, teams of teachers in other schools developed their own curriculum models for average students through the HUMANITAS program.

Three teachers' centers have been set up at schools for visits from new teacher teams from other schools. With teams in thirty-six of the district's fifty-two comprehensive high schools, the program has taken hold in this enormous and enormously diverse school system. Average students are doing above-average work, finding an academic "home" among peers and teachers in the program, attending school, completing assignments, and planning on higher education.

HUMANITAS Programs

• HUMANITAS teachers' centers have been established at three high schools, where veteran teams of teachers demonstrate interdisciplinary, thematic teaching for visiting teams from other schools. The week-long visits allow teachers to observe firsthand how philosophy, science, literature, and history are woven together. Teachers' center faculty consistently make reference to what students are learning in other classes. Exams and writing assignments probe complex topics for which students must draw on all subjects to compose their responses. Students often experience shared classes, where the classroom is that of a community of learners, teachers and students trusting in one another and learning together.

• Academic alliances with California universities include a project with UCLA on the use of portfolios for student assessment and a project to develop materials for a 1992 Los

Angeles exhibition with the Emma Goldman Library at the University of California at Berkeley.

• Cultural collaborations with arts organizations in and around Los Angeles enable students and teachers to attend art exhibitions, concerts, theater events, and community arts programs relevant to major themes in twentieth-century thought and culture they are studying. In a joint venture with the Los Angeles Music Center Opera, 1100 HUMANITAS students at twenty-four schools are producing and performing a contemporary opera written for them.

• The Media Arts Mobilization Project immerses students in areas of independent filmmaking, video, and photographic art forms. Guided by professional artists, students direct and produce media works exploring themes from the curricula developed by HUMANITAS teachers. Student productions involve intensive work to learn how to convey important visual ideas, to revise and edit, and to work productively in groups. As one student put it, "You need to weed through ten tons of bad tape to extract one good minute."

• Summer Academies, held at various local colleges and universities, offer five- to ten-day institutes for teachers consisting of workshops and panel discussions on topics such as "Multiculturalism in Education and the Arts: How Far?" and "Mexico: Splendor of Thirty Centuries." Teachers also use this time to develop their thematic ideas for the classroom and to study critical thinking methods.

HUMANITAS Collaborators and Supporters

The Ahmanson Foundation	The Pew Charitable Trusts
California Arts Council	The Rockefeller Foundation

For further information contact:

Dr. Judy Johnson, LAEP Program Director
HUMANITAS—Los Angeles Educational Partnership
315 West Ninth Street, Suite 1110
Los Angeles, CA 90015
Telephone: 213–622-5237
Fax: 213–629-5288

INHABITING OTHER LIVES
Dade County, Florida Public Schools

INHABITING OTHER LIVES is designed to create a multicultural curriculum that will help overcome racial and ethnic barriers and conflicts among students.

The Story of INHABITING OTHER LIVES

Former Dade County Superintendent Joseph Fernandez asked the Rockefeller Foundation representatives if an arts and humanities program could assist in reducing racial and ethnic conflict in the schools. Through the schools' close partnership with the United Teachers of Dade, a joint program was designed to bring communities and students together to focus on multiethnic literatures, histories, arts, and ideas. The strong joint decision-making agreement between the school administration and the teachers' union resulted in a program that is not only teacher-centered, but is also directed by teachers working out of the Dade-Monroe Teacher Education Center.

The Dade Community Foundation assists the Teacher Education Center in drawing on the expertise of universities, ethnic cultural groups, museums, and other agencies and institutions throughout the region.

The pilot programs developed by teachers and schools help to inform emerging thinking about multicultural curricula districtwide and at all levels.

INHABITING OTHER LIVES Programs

• Four-week summer institutes at Florida International University provide opportunities for teachers to discover and explore a range of creative works in literature, the arts, and music from the many rich and diverse cultures represented in Dade County schools. The 1992 institute, "Weaving Cultures and Contact in the Curriculum," combined indepth study of and visits to many multicultural expressions represented in the Greater Miami community. Consultants and presenters included local authors, artists, musicians, and writers. A parallel emphasis of this institute was on curriculum writing and specific classroom applications of humanities texts across disciplines. The 1991 institute, "Discovery and Encounter: Africa, Europe and the New World," takes an interdisciplinary look at the multiple cultural encounters of our continent and the Caribbean. "Living History through Literature," the 1990 institute, explored topics such as multiple images of beauty, the relationship between history and biography, and the search for truth in human experience based on group study and discussion of texts and performances.

• Retreats and follow-up study sessions for institute participants throughout the school year provide a forum for exchanging ideas and pursuing new topics in humanities teaching and learning.

• School-based grants enable teams of teachers to design programs for students based on their new cultural understanding. School projects have included student-directed, schoolwide festivals on Caribbean cultures, featuring poetry, theater, dance, and music composed by students and whole-school plans to reorganize the entire humanities curriculum.

INHABITING OTHER LIVES Collaborators and Supporters

Anti-Defamation League of B'nai B'rith
Black Archives of Greater Miami
Dade County Public Schools
Dade-Monroe Teacher Education Center
Florida International University
Historical Association of South Florida
Miami-Dade Community College
National Association for the Advancement of Colored People

The William and Tina Rosenberg Foundation
Southeast Bank, NA
Spanish American League Against Discrimination
University of Miami
United Teachers of Dade

For further information contact:

Ms. Rosa Harvey, Teacher/Trainer, Co-Project Director
Ms. Joanne Kaspert, Teacher/Trainer, Co-Project Director
INHABITING OTHER LIVES
c/o Teacher Education Center
1080 Labaron Drive
Miami Springs, FL 33166
Telephone: 305–887-2002
Fax: 305–884-8142

International Education Consortium (IEC)
St. Louis Public Schools and surrounding school districts

The **International Education Consortium** has been developed primarily to: (1) strengthen teachers' knowledge of international and multicultural literature, art, languages, and history so that they can teach children about their own heritage as well as the heritages of other civilizations important to the welfare of U.S. citizens; and (2) empower teachers with the intellectual authority to change curriculum in schools by organizing programs in collaboration with districts, universities, cultural institutions, and multinational corporations.

The IEC Story

In 1984, the Rockefeller Foundation joined with the Danforth and McDonnell-Douglas Foundations to create the International Education Consortium as a model coalition of universities and schools to promote international studies in St. Louis regional school districts. The need for such programming was felt by many as Missouri schools began to recognize that curriculum did not reflect the changes in the world and the changing demography of the United States.

Through its various programs, IEC is a national resource for quality teaching in international and multicultural studies. IEC is also working to document the relationship between teachers' knowledge of an academic discipline and effective teaching pedagogies that engage children in active learning. Through its resources, the IEC puts teachers and students in touch with scholarly and museum resources and travel-study opportunities such as Fulbright-Hays Group Study in India. The IEC programs emphasize primary resources, original texts, artifacts, and the arts as fundamental tools for understanding other cultures.

IEC Programs

• Summer institutes on topics such as "The World of Islam," "The End of the Cold War?" and "The Classics and the Canon: Multiculturalism."

• One-day conferences during the school year for elementary and secondary teachers that expand on themes and topics from the summer institutes.

• Curriculum design for eight units on international and multicultural literature.

• Teacher-led reading seminars in the literatures and histories of other cultures and the diverse ethnic groups of the United States.

• A resource center featuring video cassettes, books, and journals on international topics, as well as curriculum materials, available on loan to teachers throughout the region.

• A regular IEC newsletter featuring major issues in multicultural teaching.

• Long-term projects designed to institutionalize international and multicultural studies in the St. Louis Public Schools, including design of new magnet school programs, a world history revision project, and a project enabling students to strengthen their historical understanding through writing.

IEC Collaborators and Supporters

The Danforth Foundation
Hitachi Foundation
Laclede Gas Charitable Trust
James S. McDonnell Foundation
McDonnell Aircraft
Monsanto Company
National Geographic Society
  Foundation

Ralston Purina
Roblee Foundation
The Rockefeller Foundation
Southwestern Bell Foundation
DeWitt and Caroline Van Evers
  Foundation

For further information contact:

Dr. Dennis Lubeck, Executive Director
International Education Consortium
6800 Wydown Boulevard
St. Louis, MO 63105
Telephone: 314–721-3255
Fax: 314–863-0917

NEW YORK AND THE WORLD
New York City

The **NEW YORK AND THE WORLD** project is designed to accomplish four primary goals: (1) to increase appreciation of cultural diversity; (2) to develop teachers' knowledge of the literatures, histories, cultures, religions, and the arts of Africa, Latin America, Asia and the Middle East, the Soviet Union, Eastern Europe, and Western Europe in response to state mandates for Global Studies in the high schools of New York City; (3) to increase collaborative efforts between the schools and area cultural institutions in support of enhanced teaching and learning about world cultures; and (4) to increase interdisciplinary collaboration among teachers at the high-school level.

The NEW YORK AND THE WORLD Story

In 1985, the state of New York mandated that the ninth- and tenth-grade Social Studies curricula emphasize the cultures of Africa, Latin America, Asia and the Middle East, the Soviet Union, Eastern Europe, and Western Europe. Veteran teachers with little formal education in these areas found themselves ill-prepared to teach about these regions effectively.

The American Forum for Global Education, an organization specializing in teacher education in Global Studies, designed a program called NEW YORK AND THE WORLD, to increase the knowledge of teachers in Social Studies, as well as in other disciplines, of the humanities in these world areas and to design interdisciplinary curricula putting students in touch with the arts, writing, artifacts, and beliefs of the many and diverse global cultures. New York City's enormously rich museum, arts, and academic institutions join with teachers to enhance and update their knowledge of and students' experiences with world cultures. Teachers also work with colleagues to increase the use of student-centered, innovative instructional strategies, while students benefit from integrated learning experiences. NEW YORK AND THE WORLD now receives significant support from the New York City Board of Education as well as the Rockefeller Foundation.

Programs of NEW YORK AND THE WORLD

• Each school year, teachers attend a six-month intensive staff development institute surveying the humanities of one or more world areas such as sub-Saharan Africa or Latin America. Teachers develop interdisciplinary approaches to the study of these regions centered on themes such as cultural identity, values, myth, and ideology.

• Intensive day-and-a-half institutes on specific world areas, such as Turkey and the Middle East.

• Independent study grants for teachers to gather and disseminate information to fellow participants.

• Incentive grants for schools to implement NEW YORK AND THE WORLD programs.

• An annual humanities fair of student work from participating schools and their communities.

• On-site school development consultation, assisting with school restructuring and team building by NEW YORK AND THE WORLD program officers and a pool of consultants.

NEW YORK AND THE WORLD Collaborators and Supporters

American Museum of Natural History
The Americas Society
The Asia Society
The Brooklyn Museum
Citizen Exchange Council
Columbia University
The Cooper Hewitt Museum
El Museo del Barrio
Foreign Policy Association
Harriman Institute
Henry Street Settlement
Hunter College
Institute of International Education

Lehman College
The Metropolitan Museum of Art
National Museum of Design
NYC Board of Education
NYC Fund for Public Education
New York Community Trust
New York University
Queens College
The Rockefeller Foundation
The Smithsonian Institution
UNICEF
The United Nations

For further information contact:

Ms. Jaimie P. Cloud, Director for Program
NEW YORK & THE WORLD
c/o The American Forum for Global Education
45 John Street, Suite 908
New York, NY 10038
Telephone: 212–732-8606
Fax: 212–791-4132

Philadelphia Alliance for Teaching Humanities in the Schools (PATHS)
The PATHS World History Project
School District of Philadelphia

The **PATHS World History Project** has been created to achieve two primary goals: (1) to develop a new approach to World History for the School District of Philadelphia responsive to its diverse population and based on broad scholarship; and (2) to establish a continuing process for teachers' and scholars' collaborative review and revision of the World History curriculum.

The PATHS Story

In response to a 1980 study on "The Humanities in American Life," the Rockefeller Foundation, in partnership with the President's Committee on the Arts and Humanities, approached business leaders in Philadelphia with the idea of forming a coalition of businesses, foundations, universities, and cultural institutions that would work with the School District of Philadelphia to enhance arts and humanities education. This coalition, the Committee to Support Philadelphia Public Schools (CSPPS), created PATHS(The Philadelphia Alliance for Teaching Humanities in the Schools) as one of its first projects. PATHS later joined with another CSPPS project, PRISM (The Philadelphia Renaissance in Science and Mathematics). Together they formed a joint partnership in the arts and sciences, PATHS/PRISM: The Philadelphia Partnership for Education.

PATHS' first funded program, Writing Across the Curriculum, became wholly supported by the school district by 1986. At that time, the school district asked PATHS for assistance to enhance social studies education in light of a survey by the Philadelphia Federation of Teachers that made evident teachers' great dissatisfaction with the ninth-grade world history requirement. The World History Project began with scores of teachers and scholars considering the question of what they would like students to know and be able to do and how a program of study could be designed to actively engage students in that vision.

The program provides teachers and students with an approach to world history that is rooted in chronology and geography while providing a framework for the comparative study of change over time in diverse civilizations and societies. The program models the scholarly approach of the historian, and is therefore based on the study of primary sources, including literary texts and works of art. The program draws on a wealth of historical scholarship available in Philadelphia's area universities and cultural institutions. As teachers come to understand the new content and methods involved in recent historical research, they have seen a need to revise their classroom practice. The new curriculum reflects these changes and has created an evolving series of goals in writing, questioning, and cooperative learning.

Programs of the PATHS World History Project

• Staff development and curriculum development opportunities allowed teachers and scholars to work together extensively for several years, producing a sophisticated new approach to world history teaching and learning in which students are encouraged to think and act like historians. The curriculum blends theme with chronology, referring to examples of early cities, empires, religions, trade, revolutions, and technology from the perspectives of cultures on all continents.

• Teachers explore new ways of assessing student achievement in terms of inquiry, interpretation, and use of content.

• Teachers create hands-on classroom materials featuring documents and artifacts, such as models of early human skulls, fibers and ores, and art and literature, all of which students may work with directly to generate their own historical questions and hypotheses.

PATHS Collaborators and Supporters

National Geographic Society
The Pew Charitable Trusts
Philadelphia College of Textiles & Science
Philadelphia Federation of Teachers
The Rockefeller Foundation

School District of Philadelphia
Temple University
The University Museum
University of Penbnsylvania

For further information contact:

Ms. Linda D. Fredrich
Team Coordinator
PATHS/PRISM: The Philadelphia Partnership for Education
United Way Building
7 Ben Franklin Parkway, Suite 700
Philadelphia, PA 19103–1294
Telephone: 215–665-1400
Fax: 215–864-2494

Rural Education Alliance for Collaborative Humanities (REACH)
Rural South Carolina Public School Districts

The **REACH** project is designed to strengthen rural education in South Carolina through writing and the study of local history and culture. Teachers are supported in their efforts by: (1) collaborations with colleges and universities, historical societies, arts councils, museums, and other cultural organizations, artists and scholars; (2) creating new relationships among students of diverse abilities and cultures, and between the schools and their communities; and (3) designing new methods of student assessment that both inform and encourage learning as they describe student progress.

The REACH Story

As director of the Program in Writing at the Bread Loaf School of English in Vermont, Dixie Goswami, professor of English at Clemson University, had successfully worked with rural teachers throughout the country to improve their teaching of writing. Inspired by her pioneering efforts, the South Carolina Humanities Council offered to serve as official sponsor and fiscal agency for a statewide, school/college collaborative for strengthening the teaching and learning of the humanities in rural schools. With a grant from the Rockefeller Foundation in 1987, the Rural Education Alliance for Collaborative Humanities (REACH) was created, and its administrative headquarters was established in the English department at Clemson University.

Through its innovative work in many schools around the state, and through its brokering of collaborations among schools, colleges, and cultural organizations, REACH has grown to be a catalyst in South Carolina for school-based change through improvement of humanities teaching, collaboration via electronic networks, and statewide leadership for curriculum and testing reform. As REACH has developed, it has become a major link among people and institutions dedicated to education.

REACH helped to launch the South Carolina Curriculum Congress in partnership with the State Department of Education, the Commission on Higher Education, the Governor's Office, and Lander University. The South Carolina Curriculum Congress has been formed to bring educators from districts, universities, state education agencies, business, and the community together to reform curriculum and set standards across the arts and sciences. The South Carolina Curriculum Congress, linked via REACH to the Alliance for Curriculum Reform, is responsible for gathering the best knowledge of curriculum practice and building a consensus about what students should know and be able to do. From that consensus, state curriculum frameworks will be developed to guide local school curriculum innovation, teacher education programs, professional development opportunities, new forms of assessment, and other components of the educational system.

The REACH Programs

• **REACH School Programs** throughout rural South Carolina support such projects as Pickens High School's "Coming Home: A Project to Discover Community" and the Branchville Public Schools' project on "The Tracks of Time," in which students created research projects on the history, lifestyles, and climate of this community along a railroad line.

• **South Carolina Network for Educational Telecomputing**, an electronic network linking teachers, students, scholars, and others across the state and nation into an interactive learning community for educational dialogues, research collaborations, and information searches.

• **South Carolina's Cultural Memory**, a summer institute series in which the cultures of South Carolina are the focus of intensive staff development for teachers. The program is coordinated by the Institute for Southern Studies at the University of South Carolina collaboration with Clemson University and South Carolina State College.

• REACH functions in close collaboration with an alliance of project and initiatives supported by the Bingham Trust. These include the Bread Loaf School of English Writing Grants program, the Clemson Writing in the Schools programs, and the South Carolina Cross-Age Tutoring Project.

> "South Carolina Cross-Age Tutoring" is a program in which students learn by having to teach, resulting in improved literacy, a rise in self-esteem, development of a sense of responsibility, a shared sense of community, and an awareness of academic opportunities.

> Within the Clemson Writing in the Schools project, "Writing and Performing Across Cultures" is a program that uses improvisation and drama-based activities to motivate students and to strengthen their writing.

> "Writing for the Community" is a program that involves students in collecting, analyzing, and rewriting public documents, giving students a chance to see firsthand what it means to write clearly and to understand the consequences of ineffective writing.

REACH Collaborators and Supporters

BellSouth Foundation
Benedict College
Bread Loaf School of English
Clemson University
Coastal Carolina College
College of Charleston
Francis Marion College
Lander University
The Rockefeller Foundation
Showa Denko Carbon, Inc.

South Carolina Commission
 on Higher Education
South Carolina Governor's Office
South Carolina State University
 South Carolina Humanities Council
South Carolina Public Schools
South Carolina State Department
 of Education
University of South Carolina
Winthrop University

For further information contact:

Mr. Jack Blodgett, Executive Director
Project REACH
320 Daniel Hall
Clemson University
Clemson, SC 29634–1503
Telephone: 803–656-5402
Fax: 803–656-0258

Renaissance Outreach Alliance for the Detroit Area Schools (ROADS)
Detroit Area Public Schools (Wayne, Oakland, and Macomb Counties)

The **ROADS** project was developed in 1989 to: (1) strengthen humanities education in Detroit-area schools by providing teachers with quality, content-oriented programs that foster curriculum change and improved student achievement; (2) foster collaborative relationships among elementary, middle, and high-school teachers, librarians, museum professionals, and university scholars; and (3) assist educators in the development of effective teaching strategies through multicultural and interdisciplinary elements to strengthen their understanding of history, language and literature, comparative religion, the arts, and cultural geography.

The ROADS Story

ROADS is administered by the Michigan Humanities Council, an independent, non-profit organization dedicated to enriching the lives of Michigan resident through exploration and celebration of the humanities. From its experience in designing intensive professional development programs and its knowledge of humanities resources, the Michigan Humanities Council strives to design and implement a program of service to schools. The ROADS project brings together teacher to explore the history and culture of several ethnic groups and collaborate on the development of enriched curricula. Central to the project is the use of community resources and cultural institutions. Through its Symposia Series, Summer Institutes and Mini-Grant Awards, ROADS provides teachers with the opportunity to make positive, permanent changes in their schools' curricula and improve achievement in average and at-risk students.

ROADS Programs

- Summer institutes, symposia, and programs centered on a major culture, such as:
    African and African-American Heritage
    Middle Eastern Cultures
    The Americas: Hispanic History and Cultures
- Mini-grants provide area educators with resources needed to develop and implement special curricular projects related to current ROADS program cultural themes.
- Alliance-building to seek out institutional, corporate, foundation, and community support for ROADS.
- Sponsorship of a statewide humanities and education conference.
- Emphasis on the role of the arts and humanities in Professional Development Schools and other building-based reforms.

ROADS Collaborators and Supporters

Arab Community Center for Economic
and Social Services (ACCESS)
Casa De Unidad
Detroit Historical Department
Detroit Institute of Arts
Detroit Public Library
Detroit Public Schools
Eastern Michigan University
Henry Ford Museum & Greenfield
Village
Jewish Community Council of
Metropolitan Detroit
Latin Americans for Social and
Economic Development (La Sed)

Macomb Intermediate School District
Michigan Humanities Council
Michigan Ethnic Heritage Studies
Center
Michigan Geographic Alliance
Michigan State University
Museum of African American History
National Endowment for the Humanities
Oakland University
University of Detroit/Mercy
University of Michigan
Wayne County Regional Educational
Services Agency
Wayne State University

For further information contact:

Dr. Ronald Means,
Executive Director
Michigan Humanities Council
119 Pere Marquette Drive, Suite 3B
Lansing, MI 48912–1231
Telephone: 517–372–7770
Fax: 517–372–0027

Scholars United for Multicultural Inquiry in Teaching (SUMMIT)
Denver, Boulder Valley, Cherry Creek, and Douglas County Schools in the Denver metropolitan area, and Centennial School in southern Colorado.

The **SUMMIT** project is designed primarily to: (1) develop multicultural curricula to define school and district restructuring; and (2) focus curriculum on "The Five Colorados," the cultural history and development of the Native American, Chicano/Latino American, Asian American, African American and European American cultures of the region.

The SUMMIT Story

The Denver Public Education Coalition had been working in partnership with the Denver, Boulder Valley, Cherry Creek, and Douglas County school systems to provide programs in writing, restructuring, small grants to teachers, and other programs to enhance community support for improved education. The schools' needs to develop a multicultural curriculum coincided with a need to rethink the structures of schools, since multiculturalism may mean a reconsideration not only of what we teach, but also how we teach, and how school structures need to change to support new kinds of teaching.

The goals of SUMMIT, the newest CHART project, are to foster engagement among students in elementary, middle, and high-school classrooms with multicultural arts, writing, history, and other humanities, while empowering teachers to create new and more effective ways of presenting a multicultural curriculum. Since the students and teachers all share the rich ethnic heritage of Colorado, the study of its history and cultural background will form the basis for curriculum development. Encouraging a spirit of inquiry in both teachers and students is of primary importance to SUMMIT, as is the belief that increasing teachers' knowledge of a subject will serve to enhance not only the teacher's intellectual curiosity, but also, in turn, the students'.

Summer institutes immerse teachers from all five districts in alternative perspectives from the arts and literatures of the five Colorado cultures, bringing teachers closer in touch with the cultural contexts of their students. Grants to schools will challenge teachers to reorganize their curricula and school structures to accommodate new approaches.

SUMMIT Programs
• Summer Institutes for teachers:

"Earth, Water, Spirit"—a week of "cultural immersion" in San Luis, Colorado (just north of the New Mexico border) consisting of lectures, site visits, hands-on art projects, and performances, with an emphasis on curriculum development.

"Museum Hop"—a one week program working with museum educators from Denver's major and minority cultural institutions to establish direct relationships with educators and explore new methods for using museums to expand student learning in the spirit of research and inquiry.

• Grants to schools for teams of teachers to develop new curricula.

• Assistance to schools to restructure in line with new approaches developed by teachers.

SUMMIT Collaborators and Supporters

The Black American West Museum
and Heritage Center
Boulder Valley School District
Cherry Creek School District
Colorado College
Colorado Endowment for the Humanities
Colorado Historical Society
The Denver Art Museum
The Denver Center for the
Performing Arts
The Denver Children's Museum
The Denver Museum of Natural History
Denver Public Schools

Douglas County Schools
Education Commission
of the States
Metropolitan State College
Museum of Western Art
Public Education Coalition
Regis University
University of Colorado –
Boulder
University of Colorado –
Denver

For further information contact:

Mr. Patricio Córdova
Public Education Coalition
1410 Grant Street, Suite A101
Denver, CO 80203
Telephone: 303–861–8661
Fax: 303–861–1501

Superintendent's Academy for Humanities and Arts Teaching
District of Columbia Public Schools

The **Superintendent's Academy for Humanities and Arts Teaching** is a joint effort of the District of Columbia Public Schools, the Smithsonian Institution's Office of Elementary and Secondary Education, Washington, D.C.-area universities, and private organizations. The Academy develops and supports humanities- and arts-based programs that are designed to reduce the dropout rate in the public school system.

The Academy Story

In 1989, the superintendent of schools in the District of Columbia began efforts to keep students in school by addressing problems that had been identified by research into dropout rates and behaviors. While African Americans make up over 60 percent of the District's population, an overwhelming 98 percent of those who leave school are African American. The research suggested that these students tend to become disaffected with school in the junior high school years. To help these students find themselves in the curriculum, the superintendent initiated the Academy to develop model curricula in African American studies.

The Academy enhances teachers' knowledge of the rich cultural heritage of African Americans by drawing on the resources of a variety of Washington, D.C.-based cultural institutions such as the Smithsonian Institution. Teachers learn about the literature and other arts of African Americans from artists, writers, professors, museum specialists, and leading figures in the national African American community during school year institutes and intensive summer programs. Each school develops its own curriculum, emphasizing interdisciplinary study and students' active learning. The new curricula link class activities with students' out-of-school experiences, adding a new perspective to student's artistic and cultural heritage.

Academy Programs

The Academy programs include summer institutes for teachers and grants to schools to help teams of teachers develop model curricula in African American studies. Examples of model programs include:

• An art studio, "Kente Kids Room," that allows students to study African and African-American art and learn techniques for creative expression.

• A history and architecture investigation, "Project Let's Go," that studies the role of African Americans and Hispanics in the development of the nation's capitol.

These and other school projects designed by teacher teams include reading and writing essays and poetry about ancient and modern African cultures, African-American history, literature, music, theater, and dance. They also include learning about the achievements of African American mathematicians, inventors, and other contributors in scientific fields.

Academy Collaborators and Supporters

Chesapeake and Potomac Telephone Company

Church of God In Christ, Inc.

Community Foundation of Greater Washington

The District of Columbia Department of Recreation

Howard University

The Kennedy Center for the Performing Arts

The National Science Foundation

The Naval District of Washington

Potomac Power and Electric Company (PEPCO)

Riggs National Bank

The Rockefeller Foundation

The Smithsonian Institution Office of Elementary and Secondary Education

The Hattie M. Strong Foundation

Trinity College

The United Black Fund

The University of the District of Columbia

The Washington Informer

For further information contact:

Ms. Maria Marable
The Smithsonian Institution
Office of Elementary and Secondary Education
Arts & Industry Building, Room 1163, MRC402
Washington, DC 20560
Telephone: 202–357-1697
Fax: 202–357-2116